In the Reign of Peace

HUGH NISSENSON

In the Reign
of Peace

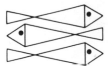

FARRAR, STRAUS & GIROUX

New York

Copyright © 1968, 1969, 1970, 1972 by Hugh Nissenson
All rights reserved
Library of Congress catalog card number: 71–179794
ISBN 0–374–17657–4
First printing, 1972
Published simultaneously in Canada by
Doubleday Canada Ltd., Toronto
Printed in the United States of America
Designed by Dorris Huth

Some of these stories originally appeared in somewhat different form in the following magazines: "In the Reign of Peace"
in *Harper's Magazine;* "The Crazy Old Man," "Charity," and
"Grace" in *Esquire;* "Forcing the End" (under the title "On
Jaffa Road") and "Going Up" in *Midstream;* and "Lamentations" in *The New Yorker*

For Kate
and once again as always for Marilyn

Contents

The Son of David will come when one
generation of man is either totally
guilty or totally innocent.

—THE BABYLONIAN TALMUD

The Throne
of Good

DECEMBER 12, 1946. ARI ROSENBERG, WHO I NOW realize is a member of the Stern gang, has made an appeal to my professional conscience. A sixteen-year-old boy his organization has somehow managed to smuggle into the country from a British detention camp in Cyprus has fallen ill.

"I think it's pneumonia," says Rosenberg.

"What're his symptoms?"

"You'd better have a look at him yourself," he tells me, and lowering his voice even though my office is empty, adds, "He's here in Tel Aviv. I've got him hidden in the cellar of an empty house on Hebron Street, near the Old Cemetery. He hasn't been out of there in three weeks."

"In this weather?"

"That's what worries me. He has a Primus stove, but we have had a hard time supplying him with enough fuel. The C.I.D. and the Haganah are on our necks right now, and we've got to be very careful about being followed. Unheated, that place is as cold and damp as a tomb. Will you have a look at him? He's had a bad time of it."

"What about your own doctors?"

"We can't be sure they're not being watched."

Another gust of wind off the sea rattles the window above the leather chair. The glass is blurred by rain. And yet I can make out a woman huddled in the doorway across the street. She has gray hair. Is it possible that I'm under surveillance? Does the British Criminal Investigation Department employ middle-aged Jewish women as spies? It doesn't surprise me.

In any case, Rosenberg, who followed my glance, has seen her too, but says nothing. Only his expression has changed, the look in his eyes, which gleam maliciously. He has already implicated me in his activities and knows that I know it.

"What's the boy's name?" I ask.

"What's the difference?"

"Suit yourself."

He repeats, "Will you come and see him?"

"All right."

"Good. Meet me exactly at midnight tonight on the corner of Tchernichovsky and Gan Meir."

"I'll be there."

"I appreciate it." And he adds, without any irony I can detect, "For old times' sake."

But at the door, he alters his tone. "During the Vilna ghetto uprising, in the war, he took the name *Zemsta*."

"*Zemsta?*"

"Polish for 'revenge,' " Rosenberg explains.

It's taken two hours—we doubled back twice on Rothschild Boulevard—for Rosenberg to lead me to the boy's hide-out: the cellar of a small abandoned house on Hebron Street. And now I wait alone for almost ten minutes in the back yard. It's a shame, the garden has gone to hell: a single pomegranate tree, above my head, sways in the wind. All its round, reddish fruits, bursting with juicy scarlet seeds, have long since dropped in the mud and rotted away.

The outside cellar door opens a crack, and Rosenberg whispers, "Come ahead."

He has a flashlight. We carefully climb down the wooden steps into the darkness. The beam of light, flitting here and there, illuminates a small room: in one corner, an iron cot, a small table, and a Primus stove at the head of the bed, on the concrete floor. Here, the air is stifling. The bedclothes and the boy's hair reek of naphtha fumes.

The boy is suffering from bronchorrhea, characterized by a slight fever at night—now a little over 38° C.—diffuse râles, and a persistent cough which brings up a thin, purulent, yellow phlegm. As I have no antibiotics—there are none as yet available for civilians in the country—I prescribe aspirin, rest, and calcreose, 5 gr., in chocolate-coated tablets to be taken three times a day.

He asks me in excellent Hebrew, "When will I be well enough to get out of here?"

"A couple of weeks."

"You can do better than that." Racked by coughing, he is unable to continue.

"Do you want the truth?" I whisper to Rosenberg at the head of the stairs. "That boy is going to get a lot worse unless you move him out of there immediately."

"It can't be done."

"Why not?"

"Our plans are set, and we can't take a chance of having him captured. Anyway, he's a volunteer. He accepts the risk."

He hands me the flashlight and draws a British service revolver from his side pocket.

"A Webley-Fosbery," he explains. "Unreliable. A speck of dust and it jams. Still, we use whatever we can get our hands on. We have our orders, you know."

"What kind of orders?"

"Turn off that light."

He opens the door, looks out, and says, "This way."

Stuffing the revolver back into the pocket of his mackintosh, he leads me across the yard, under the pomegranate tree. The mud sucks at our shoes. Hebron Street is deserted. Huge, inert pools of water have gathered in the drainless street.

Rosenberg accompanies me home. Across Allenby Road, under a street lamp, a patrol of British paratroopers, whom our children have nicknamed "poppies" because of their red berets. Blue eyes, sandy hair, mottled, beardless cheeks: they are little more than children themselves, but they are all armed. Each one has a finger on the trigger of the Sten gun slung across his chest.

Rosenberg leads me around the corner. He is grinding his teeth together with such force that his jaw muscles bulge on the right side of his face, beside his ear. It's a habit he has retained from childhood. We grew up on the same block in Haifa, but in that dark mackintosh, with one hand thrust in a pocket gripping a gun, he has become unrecognizable to me. The bulging jaw belongs to someone else; none of our common childhood memories which might bind us together again is evoked: the smell of broiling *kebab*, mingled in the salty air with crude oil from the refineries; the one-legged Arab beggar, in black rags, sprawled on the sidewalk near the Town Hall, whom we passed every afternoon on our way home from school. Rosenberg, who was already proficient in idiomatic Arabic, would stop and chat with him. The beggar invariably refused our proffered coins.

"Why?" I once asked Rosenberg.

"Because I listen to what he has to say," he explained.

We were even in the same class at the Hebrew University, where he took a degree in Hebrew literature. I thought I knew everything about him, but realize I know nothing.

He has deliberately placed his Webley on the table between us. It has recently been oiled. Has he actually killed anyone with it? Detonated an electric mine? It's inexplicable.

He drinks off his third brandy; his eyelids droop.

"Tell me about the boy," I ask.

He yawns. "There's not much to tell. He was born in Molodechno, where his father was a grain merchant, and his mother the only daughter of a cantor in Vilna. The father did pretty well. He started the kid in *cheder* at three and wanted him to go to a yeshiva and become a rabbi. The kid was bright enough, but restless. He skipped classes and roamed the fields with the local peasants. His father begged him to study, but it wasn't any use. The old man took a strap to him more than once.

"Anyway, the whole family was deported to the Vilna ghetto in May 1941. A month later, the parents were murdered in the pogrom in the Nowograd marketplace. The kid was saved because he was studying Talmud with his grandfather at the time.

"He ran away the next day, taking a bread knife and, of all things, his father's prayer book, and joined the United Partisan Organization. The F.P.O. First he served as a courier, and then, the next spring, at the age of thirteen, he stabbed to death a Lithuanian policeman, a 'man-hunter' they used to call them, who helped the Germans round up Jews in the ghetto for extermination in Treblinka. As a result, the kid was posted to Itzik Beinisch's command on Staszuma Street, the building that was the first line of defense in the uprising against the Germans. They fought like hell but didn't stand a chance. Most of them were wiped out, except for a few hundred who somehow managed to escape to the forests outside the city or,

like the kid, were able to hide in the sewers and underground bunkers until they were liberated by the Red
Army in July of 1944."

"In the sewers?"

"In the sewers," Rosenberg repeats. "He spent almost eleven months in those sewers." He picks up his
revolver and asks, "Do you know any songs of the
Vilna partisans?"

"No."

"I'm translating some of them from Yiddish into
Hebrew. We want to bring out a Hebrew edition. But
it's hard to preserve the idiom. Do you remember any
Yiddish?"

"Some."

His bleary eyes have suddenly cleared; he recites in
an animated voice:

> *Sligt ergetz fartayet,*
> *Der feint vee a chayeh*
> *Der Mauser, er vacht in mine hant . . .*

"It's a problem," he goes on. "A literal translation is
easy: 'the enemy' . . . what? . . . 'harkens; a beast in
the darkness; the Mauser, it wakes in my hand . . .' "

Absorbed in thought, he slips on his mackintosh,
returns his revolver to his pocket, and absent-mind-

edly pats it. Is it possible that his literary imagination
—or aspirations—compels him to assume this role?
Is such a thing likely?

December 15, 1946. For the last two days, I've been
under surveillance; there's no doubt of it. First, by
that middle-aged woman lurking in the doorway
across the street, and then, as I make my daily
rounds, by a tall young man who wears a leather
jacket. Today, making no effort to conceal himself,
he followed me to the clinic on Etzion Gever, spon-
sored by the Zionist Federation of Labor.

A few Arab women from Jaffa still bring their children to be treated here for trachoma, boils, ringworm,
and chronic dysentery. The boys, particularly, amaze
me. They lie naked and motionless on the sheet, under the overhead light, never uttering a sound, while
I incise and then drain the boils that usually cover
their buttocks and the backs of their thighs. Only the
women, whom I hear through a thin partition, moan
aloud. This afternoon one of them fainted dead away.
Observing the Arab custom, I had Miss Guinzburg,
my nurse, remove her veil and bring her around with
spirits of ammonia.

Finished at five, I walk, in the rain, to the café on

Dizengoff, where I usually have a cup of Arab coffee and a brandy. Leather Jacket remains just outside. The rain has plastered his hair to his forehead and hangs in shining drops from the tip of his nose and his earlobes. As I am about to leave, a roving patrol of Royal Marines stops and carefully examines his papers. Apparently satisfied, the sergeant, who has a bristling mustache, shoos him away.

"Go on," the sergeant yells, " 'op it!" and waits until Leather Jacket has boarded a bus on the corner.

Rosenberg, in his black mackintosh, is waiting for me outside the door of my flat.

"The kid's getting worse," he says. "Much worse. Will you come and have a look at him again?"

He's clearly worried but insists on taking the usual precaution. We wander around the city for an hour and a half, until we reach the Old Cemetery and the cellar on Hebron Street. No one follows us. Apart from a solitary Arab policeman, armed with a British rifle, on Allenby Road, the flooded streets are empty. The Arab wears a *kulpack*, obligatory for native police. It's a kind of fez made from black lamb's wool. But it's much too big for him, and as he turns his head to watch us pass, it slips down to the bridge of his nose.

On the table in the cellar a flickering candle, stuck in its own grease, on an overturned glass, throws our enormous, leaping shadows on the peeling whitewashed wall.

"It's freezing down here," I tell the boy. "Do you want to catch pneumonia? Why don't you use that Primus?"

"I ran out of fuel yesterday."

"I'll try and send him some tomorrow morning," Rosenberg says.

"Then bundle up, for God's sake."

"The cold doesn't bother me," the boy says.

He is suddenly convulsed by a cough and he spits into a filthy handkerchief. The sputum now is grayish white and separated into an upper layer capped with frothy mucus and a thick sediment in which there are dirty yellow masses. He has developed putrid bronchitis.

"Well?" Rosenberg asks.

"You'd better get him to a hospital tonight."

"I can't."

"There's nothing I can do for him here."

"Don't you understand? He has forged ID papers, but the C.I.D. has a complete dossier on him. They know he's in the country. If they catch him, they'll cure him all right, but then what do you think will happen? He knows too much, but he won't talk. At least not under physical torture. But they're smart. They'll keep him in some cell in Acre."

The boy repeats, "In Acre? Underground?" He shakes his head. "No, I don't think I could take that. I've already been down here almost a month. To tell you the truth, I'm beginning to hear things."

"What kind of things?" I ask.

"A rattling chain and a growling dog. Isn't that odd? A huge, savage dog at the end of a long chain tied to the doorknob, at the head of the stairs, outside."

"It's only your fever. It'll pass."

He says, "You think so? I'm not so sure. The SS in Vilna sometimes chained vicious dogs to the gratings on the streets to prevent us from coming up at night to scrounge around the city for a bite to eat."

"Did you ever try to escape through the sewers to the forests and join the partisans?"

"I couldn't," he says. "It was *beshaert*," he adds in Yiddish. "Fated. I know that now. I was fated for other things. For a long time, I had a whatchamacallit —I don't know the word in Hebrew. You know, from a bad knock on the head."

"A concussion."

"Yes. I was on the second floor of our headquarters

on Staszuma Street, stuffing a rag into a bottle of gasoline. The Germans were attacking. There was a
bright flash, dust and plaster flying through the air,
and I suppose the ceiling fell down. I can't remember.
The next thing I know was that Shmuel Epstein, one
of Itzik's lieutenants, was carrying me on his back
through the sewers. That's very vivid. My head ached
something terrible, but I hung on, my arms wrapped
around his neck, with all my strength. He had a pillowcase, a linen pillowcase stuffed with something,
between his teeth. Once he forgot himself and opened
his mouth to speak to me, and it dropped into the filth.

" 'What's in it?' I asked him, and he said, 'Three
candles, a box of matches, two loaves of bread, and
your *siddur*.' 'Mine?' I asked him, and he told me he
found it in my jacket pocket. Can you imagine? It was
the prayer book that belonged to Papa. I always carried it around with me, after his death, and Shmuel
took the trouble to bring it along. That's the kind of
man he was. Of course, the pillowcase was soaked
through, oozing black, stinking drops. Anyway, he
held it between his teeth and kept going. The sewer
pipe was about seventy or eighty centimeters high,
and he crawled on his elbows in order not to bang my
head again. It kept aching something terrible. He
went very slowly. It was like a dream in slow motion.

First his right arm and his right leg together, then his left for . . . I don't know how long. My feet, up to the ankles, trailed behind in the slime. I remember passing the waterfall under Stephan Street. The water dropped six or eight meters there and made a terrific roar in those pipes. But gradually it faded away.

"Then Shmuel stopped. I realized he was exhausted and slipped off his back. I followed him for as long as I could, but there was a sudden rush of water, and I lost him. He was swept away before my eyes. I managed to brace my arms and legs against the pipe, or I would have drowned too. A day or so later . . . I can't be sure . . . it must have rained. The current in the sewers was very strong. I barely managed to keep my head above water.

"After that, I'm not sure what happened. I went off my head. I began seeing things. I must have been thinking about the forest, because I saw flowers growing down there, in that muck. But they were black. Can you imagine that? Spiny black stems and black petals. And then, for a time, I heard Mama calling me. It was her voice, all right. I'd know it anywhere. I'd know it right now. And it echoed, as though it were real. She'd come down to try and find me. Lead me back up. She kept calling out my name and moaning. I wanted to answer her, but I was afraid to open my mouth. I was lying back on my elbows, against the pipe, up to my chin in that slime, and I was terrified that if I opened my mouth, and a sudden current caught me, I'd drown."

He closes his eyes. "Malka Kravitz eventually found me and took me to her bunker under the cellar at 19 Deitshishe Street, where I spent the rest of the war. We even had a radio and an electric light. We used to sleep during the day, and roam around the sewers at night. Visit other bunkers. We dug a cemetery in the bunker under 9 Gelzer Street and even had a synagogue, where I used to pray. I knew I had been saved for a purpose and tried to prepare myself."

"What purpose?"

He stares at the ceiling and moistens his dry lips with the tip of his tongue.

December 16, 1946. Noon. In my office. Leather Jacket, who tells me his name is Nahum, turns out to be an agent of the Haganah. He says, "Your friend Rosenberg, you know, planned the murder of Major Henry in September."

"Henry?"

"The British area security officer."

As I doodle on my prescription pad, it all comes back to me: the shots in the night, the explosion, according to the newspapers, of two hundred kilograms of dynamite, and the smoldering debris of the villa on Levinsky Street, which I saw the next morning, where the dying major and the bodies of two Arab policemen were found.

"Was Rosenberg really responsible for that?"

"There's no question of it," he says, resting one arm on top of the locked glass cabinet where I keep my toxic drugs. Wearing rubber boots, in which he's tucked the ends of his khaki pants, he gives the impression of a cavalryman; all he needs is a braided riding crop. Or at least he tries to give that impression. He stands without grace, his huge feet too wide apart, and he has the hands of a farmer: red knuckles and dirty fingernails.

He goes on. "Henry was married, you know."

"I had no idea."

"Oh, yes. To a pretty little French girl. She was caught in the blast, of course. From what we've heard, no one knows whether she'll make it or not."

"I'm very sorry to hear it."

"I believe you. We know the kind of man you are."

"What kind is that?"

He smiles. "If you told us where the boy is hiding, we'd pick him up and put him on ice for a while, on a kibbutz in the Galilee."

"He's got a bad infection."

"Has he? Well, we've got a well-equipped infirmary, a good nurse, and a doctor who drops by from Tiberias three times a week. He'll be in good hands. I promise you."

"Is the kibbutz near Tiberias?"

"Close enough."

"Are you a member?" I ask him.

He hesitates, and then, with the air of sharing a confidence, replies, "Yes." He sniffs at his right palm. "I'm in charge of the sheep. Lord, what a stink! You can never get rid of it."

"Rosenberg is armed, you know," I tell him. "He won't be taken alive."

"We have no intention of tangling with him, or any other Jew, unless we have to. Is the boy armed?"

"No, I don't think so."

"Good." He goes to the window and peers down. "God only knows what they're cooking up this time."

I rise and follow him. The middle-aged woman across the street is smoking a cigarette. Nahum says,

"Don't worry about Rosenberg. We'll keep an eye on him. When you make up your mind to tell us where the boy is hiding, tell Guela down there."

It's begun to drizzle. The gray-haired woman steps back into the doorway and turns up the collar of her blue coat.

December 18, 1946. I've returned to the cellar alone. The door is unlocked, and my wet shoes squeak as I carefully make my way down the stairs. It suddenly occurs to me that the boy may now have a gun. I pause and strike a match. A brown rat scurries between my feet. The match goes out.

"It's Doctor Spitzer," I call out. "Remember? Rosenberg's friend. I'm all alone. I came by to see how you're coming along."

The boy answers in a hoarse voice, "Of course. Come on down."

"I can't see a damn thing."

"Wait a minute, I'll light my candle," he says. "Come over here and warm up."

Wrapped in his blanket, he is hunched over on the edge of his cot, rubbing his hands over the hissing Primus.

"How's this for service?" he asks, thumping his shoe against a jerrican on the floor. "British Army-issue gasoline for the stove. Two of our girls stole it last night from an army lorry waiting for a green light on Ben Yehuda."

"Lie down and let me have a look at you."

He shakes his head. "No, what's the sense? I'll be leaving here in a day or two anyway, maybe less."

"Leaving?"

"Orders," he says, and asks, "Have you ever killed a man face to face with your bare hands?"

"No."

He coughs into his handkerchief. "I stabbed a Lithuanian man-hunter, you know, when I was thirteen. With a bread knife I always carried on me, under my shirt, stuck in my belt . . ."

Pale, sweaty, completely enervated, he lies back with his hands behind his head. His chest is distended. But then he resumes talking with the same passion as before, as if his memory alone remains inexhaustible.

"I stabbed him in the stomach, face to face, in an alley just off Rudnitzer Street, at night. A beautiful spring night, with a full moon. I could see everything. There I was, turning the corner, with a message for

Itzik in my pocket, and he was standing there, light-
ing a cigarette. He had very bushy blond eyebrows,
I remember.

"It was all over in a second. I didn't give him a
chance. I threw myself at him and stuck the bread
knife into his guts, right up to the hilt. He didn't make
a sound. Then I pulled it out, very slowly, and let him
have it again. He was already on his knees, holding
on to the hilt with both hands. The blood seeped between his fingers. It looked black. Then he fell on his
face. His peaked cap rolled off his head. He was wearing a white arm band, by the way, all the man-
hunters did. I don't know why."

He coughs again and spits on the floor. "Then I
started running. It was a stupid thing to do. I should
have taken his pistol. We had almost no weapons. But
I got scared, I suppose, and ran like hell until I got
back to Itzik and gave him the message. 'You're all
covered with blood,' he said. 'Yes,' I told him, 'I
stabbed a man-hunter to death in an alley off Rudnitzer Street.'

"He put his arm around me. 'Never mind,' he said.
'You'll get used to it after a while.' 'Used to it?' I said,
and I looked at the sadness on his face; on all the
other faces, too. The same grief.

" 'Give me something to drink,' I told them. 'Haven't

we got a drop of schnapps left around here?' Itzik passed me a bottle of Polish vodka, the best, with the blade of grass in it. I took three solid swigs, and it went right to my head. The real stuff.

" 'Come on,' I said. 'For God's sake, this is a celebration. Drinks all around. Who knows a song?'

"But what did they do? Stared at me, open-mouthed. 'Well, I do,' I told them." And raising himself up on his elbows, he sings a verse in Yiddish, clapping his hands.

"Do you understand it?" he asks me and, without waiting for an answer, translates it into Hebrew in his hoarse voice:

> Heavy sheaves full of wheat,
> Full of cheerful songs.
> And the sun, it burns like fire.
> Every hour is precious to us.
> The field has given us bread
> For the beautiful new life.

Then he lies back again, gasping for breath. "I took another couple of healthy swigs from that bottle. Wonderful stuff. I swear it smelled of that grass. The next thing I remember was waking up, in a corner, in Yankele's arms. We called him 'The Rebbe.' He was a yeshiva bocher, about seventeen, who'd joined us about a week before. When he wasn't running messages like me, he was praying.

" 'Do you feel better?' he asked me.

" 'Me? I never felt better in my life,' I told him. 'I stabbed him twice, you know. And when I pulled the knife out the first time, he grabbed the blade and cut his fingers.'

" 'Is that so?' Yankele said. He scratched the back of his neck—we were all crawling with lice—and asked me, 'Do you know what the Besht, may his memory protect us, once said?' And he leaned forward and whispered in my ear, 'Evil is only the throne of good.' "

"And is that what you believe?" I ask the boy.

"It's true," he says. "How can you deny it?"

December 19, 1946. It's done. I've betrayed the boy's hide-out. This morning I had a few words with poor Guela, who's caught a bad head cold from lurking in that doorway.

"You'd better move tonight," I tell her. "They're up to something."

She sneezes and, with her nose in a handkerchief, turns on her heel toward Allenby, but I stop her. "Do you have the address of my flat?"

"Of course."

"Then ask Nahum to drop by when it's all over, will you?"

She nods, and it's the café on Dizengoff for me, where I order a pint of Johnnie Walker Red, which I can't afford. Two agents of the C.I.D. are seated at the next table, to my right, wearing identical clothes: gray flannel trousers and single-breasted blue tweed jackets that bulge from the revolvers they carry in shoulder holsters against their hearts. One of them orders two glasses of whisky, with a siphon of soda, in a Hebrew which his thick Manchester accent renders almost unintelligible. The waiter, who is a survivor of Sachsenhausen, pretends not to understand and shrugs.

"The bloody Yid," the agent says in English.

"Forget it," the other one says. "Needn't make a moan of it." He's older, wearier, with a drawn sallow face. "To hell wi' him. Let's pack it in. It's been a long day."

At the door, they put on their trench coats. It's raining again, as if to console them with a memory of home.

Maybe it's the Scotch; I've already had three stiff drinks, but I can't help feeling a twinge of pity for them. A working knowledge of Hebrew entitles them to a bonus of five pounds sterling a month, and from the look of their frayed collars and cuffs, they can use it.

1 p.m. In my flat. Nahum is seated on the chair under the bookshelf with his head in his hands. He's soaked to the skin, and his rubber boots are covered with mud, which he has tracked on my Persian carpet.

"The boy's gone," he says. "Vanished." He looks up. "Do you have something for a headache? My head's splitting."

"What happened?"

"A fuck-up, a complete fuck-up, from beginning to end. Just one of those things. We'd posted a lookout on Hebron Street, opposite the house, to keep an eye out for Rosenberg. Just a kid, but a damn police mobile force, cruising around, picked him up for routine questioning. They took him to the police station on Jaffa Street, checked his papers, which were all in order, of course, asked him a few questions, and then let him go. But by that time, it was too late. Eli and I . . . you don't know Eli, do you? No, of course not. He served in the night squads with Wingate in '37 . . . Anyway, we arrived at Hebron Street at exactly 10 p.m., as we'd planned. The lookout, of course, wasn't there, but we decided to take a chance. We went into the back yard, but I knew something was wrong. The cellar door was wide open, banging in the wind. Eli shined his flashlight down there, but the place was empty. A cot, a table, a Primus, and a jerrican of gasoline. There was a rat on the table gnawing on a candle. The boy was gone.

"Rosenberg's no fool. My guess is that he must have hidden himself in the cemetery and, when he saw our lookout picked up, ran back to the cellar, wrapped the boy up in a blanket—there was no blanket on the cot —and took him away. And now he's on the loose."

"He needs medical attention. He won't get far without it."

"Rosenberg'll manage it somehow. You can bet on it. He's got special plans for that boy."

He shuts his eyes and rubs his forehead. "I hate to bother you, but my head is splitting wide open."

He drinks the bromide I mix for him in the kitchen and then repeats, "He's loose."

December 21, 1946. 7:30 p.m. Clear weather since early morning, but now it's clouding up. I've decided to return to Hebron Street, and for the first time by the shortest route: up Allenby Road.

The street is jammed; the crowd in an ugly mood. In a café on the corner of Brenner Street, behind a streaked window, a ranting middle-aged man bangs his fist on a table. The whole town seems possessed by an unsubstantiated rumor that a French freighter, chartered by the Haganah and crammed with over six hundred "illegal" Jewish refugees, has been intercepted in the Aegean and escorted to Cyprus.

In any case, the C.I.D. is making a show of force, along with the British and Arab constabulary. They range up and down the street, with drawn revolvers, demanding I D papers from screaming Jews who are made to stand with their hands raised while being frisked.

For some reason, the British have gotten it into their heads that members of the Stern gang have taken to disguising themselves as religious Jews. In the middle of the next block, in front of a pharmacy, a ruddy-faced British policeman wearing a soft peaked cap is carefully examining, page by page, a thick tractate of the Talmud for concealed copies of *The Front*, the propaganda pamphlet of the Stern gang that is generally distributed by fifteen- or sixteen-year-old kids. The bearded old man to whom the book belongs wrings his hands.

Hebron Street is dark and quiet. I stand in the

muddy back yard. The cellar door creaks on its rusty hinges and is abruptly thrown open by a gust of wind. All that comes to mind is Nahum's repeated whisper, filled with horror, as he wiped the bromide from his lips, "He's loose . . ."

And then I imagine the boy, wrapped in that blanket reeking of naphtha, emerging from underground and disappearing into the darkness above. Where is he, I wonder? Has Rosenberg managed to smuggle him out of town?

I start back home, past the Old Cemetery, down Ben Yehuda and Allenby. The streets are littered with sodden scraps of paper. In front of The Lord Nelson, a bar particularly popular with British N.C.O.'s, the owner—a fat South African Jew—has dragged a case of imported Guinness stout out on the sidewalk, and bending over, he solemnly smashes the full bottles, one by one, against the curb. The crowd, which has grown considerably, watches in silence.

A British armored car is now parked at the intersection of Allenby and Hess. It swivels its turret, from which the barrel of a machine gun protrudes, toward a young girl with disheveled blond hair shaking her furled umbrella in the air.

"He's loose . . ."

Is it conceivable that any good can come of it?

The Crazy
Old Man

THE OLD MAN IS STILL ALIVE, LIVING IN THE same apartment on Jaffa Road in Jerusalem. He's very old by now, in his late eighties, blinded by a cataract in his left eye, but when I saw him last, about a week after the liberation of the Old City, he was on his way, alone, to pray at the Wall. He recognized me immediately—or so I thought—but after a few minutes' conversation on the street I realized that he confused me with Uzi because he asked if I still lived in Haifa. I let it pass, and chatted for a while. He still lived with his daughter, he said, who was married to a captain in the paratroops, and had two children. His son-in-law had fought and been wounded in the fight for the Old City, making a dash across the crest of the Temple Mount toward the Dome of the Rock.

"What's his name?" I asked.

"Seligman."

"Raphael?" I asked, and he answered in Yiddish, "Yes. You know him?"

"We've met."

He peered at me with his good eye; at my unshaven face and civilian clothes—a filthy white shirt and blue trousers I was wearing for an Intelligence job I'd just finished in the Old City.

"So you know Raphael," he said.

"He's a good soldier."

"Is he?"

"Where was he hit?" I asked.

"In the arm. Nothing. A flesh wound in the muscle up here."

Up to then I thought that I had detected pride in his voice and that he had at last recovered his sanity. But then he said, "I must go and pray for him now, and ask forgiveness."

And off he went, wearing a black felt hat with a wide brim, a long black gabardine coat, and those knee-length white stockings. In his right hand he carried a ragged, blue velvet bag embroidered with a gold Star of David, for his prayer shawl. He was the same.

Nothing had changed for him in almost twenty years. I resisted an impulse to run upstairs to take a look at his apartment, imagining that that, too, had remained the same, with its wicker chairs and that hideous sideboard made from teak and inlaid with mother-of-pearl that he had bought from some Arab when he first came to the country from Russia in 1912. Instead, I strolled up King George Street and, to get out of the sun, had a cup of bitter coffee in an immaculate German café.

Later in the afternoon, driving back to G.H.Q. in Tel Aviv, I thought about the whole thing for the first time in years, watching the stream of Dan buses, private cars, captured Jordanian Ford trucks with Arab license plates, and even a Russian jeep taken from the Syrians, all packed with people heading for the Wall. The rest of the Old City was still closed to civilians because of snipers and mines. I thought about Uzi, who died in 1953 in a car accident on the Tel Aviv–Haifa road, and the two Arab prisoners.

At the time, in July 1948, during the Ten Days' Fighting just before the second truce, Uzi and I were with the Haganah's Intelligence in Jerusalem, assigned to interrogate prisoners and gather information for the coordinated attack that was to be made on the Old City.

The plan was simple: a simultaneous break-through from the north through the New Gate by a unit of the Irgun, and from the south, by the Haganah, near the Zion Gate. The Old City wall is four yards thick here, but we had high hopes that we'd be able to breach it with a new explosive that we had never tried before. As it turned out, the stuff hardly scratched the wall's surface, and the plan failed. So, in the end, what we did was useless.

Uzi and I had been detailed to find out the exact number and disposition of the Arab forces around the Zion Gate from two Jordanian legionnaires who had been captured the day before. We had twelve hours to get the information out of them, so we took them to my apartment, which I had used as a "drop" for ammunition during the Mandate and where I now did most of my work. It was one room on the second floor, right across the hall from the old man and his daughter. They didn't bother me much. The old man was busy praying, and the girl, who was about twelve or thirteen, was very shy. Only once, in the last month of the Mandate, the old man invited me into his apartment for a glass of tea.

"I insist," he told me. "The kettle's on the stove. There, you hear? Already boiling. Sit down. I have no lemon. Sugar?"

"Thanks."

"Enough?"

"One more. Yes, that's fine, thanks."

"Keep the spoon. I have one here." He blew into his steaming glass and, with a spoonful of sugar already on his tongue, took a sip and smacked his lips. "Ah. That's a pleasure. Sugar on the tongue." He smiled. "For me, it somehow never tastes as good in the glass. A habit from the Old Country. But you, of course, were born here, weren't you?"

"Yes, in Tel Aviv."

"Tel Aviv. Is that so?" He stroked his red beard streaked with gray. "You're lucky."

"You think so?"

"I know so. You see, this is your chance. Not mine. Not an old Jew like me who came here to pray for forgiveness and die, but yours. My daughter Chanele's and yours, if you understand me."

"Thanks for the tea, but I have to go out. It's almost curfew."

"No, no, wait. Just one minute. You must listen to me for just one minute and try to understand." He suddenly began to sweat. His forehead, wrinkled with concentration, glistened. "The Exile, you see, the real Exile is that we learned to endure it," he suddenly went on. "Rabbi Hanokh, may he rest in peace,

once said that, and he was right. But it's all over now.
I can feel it. I look at you and even my little Chanele,
my shy little Chanele, who dreams of becoming a
courier for the Haganah . . . Can you believe that?
It's true. At twelve. That pious child . . . All of you
who were born here have had enough and will have
your State. For you, the Exile is over. Not that it
wasn't deserved." He wagged a forefinger. "Oh, no.
Never for one moment think that. We sinned and
were punished for it. It was just. But He has relented,
you see, may His Name be blessed forever and ever,
and, in His mercy, has given you one more chance.
So you must be careful. Very, very careful.

"No, please, sit down," he said, and in a lower voice
went on. "When I was a boy ten years old, there was
a pogrom in my town. A little town south of Kiev,
and a little pogrom. Ten, twelve Jews killed, and
three wounded. Nothing extraordinary, except that
a Russian blacksmith raped and murdered a Jewish
woman he had known for forty years. They had
grown up together. Played together as children. His
name was Kolya. Huge and gentle, with his eyebrows
and eyelashes all burned away from the sparks that
flew from his forge. After *cheder,* I would go and
watch him work and sometimes he'd even share his

food with me—his only meal of the day. *Talakno,* a kind of porridge made from oats and mixed with cold water. We ate from the same dish with long wooden spoons. But I saw him do it. With my own eyes, from a window in our cellar, to Sarah, who was a grandmother, the wife of Mulya the tailor. Then, while I watched, Kolya strangled her with those huge hands. I saw it all, and I learned a secret. He was human. Kolya was a human being, just like little Itzik the *shammis,* for example, or myself. There was no question of that. But he was different. And what was the difference? His violence. Violence made all the difference between us, the goyim and the Jews." He leaned toward me. His breath smelled of cloves. "And let me tell you something else," he whispered. "The Holocaust . . . Why did He relent and save a remnant from the ovens and bring them here? I'll tell you why. Because they didn't fight back."

"I've got to go," I told him. "I've got a meeting. We've just gotten a shipment of some Czech rifles."

In any case, as I said, we had twelve hours to get the information from the prisoners. It wasn't much time. We started in about nine at night, working them over according to the system that Uzi and I had found to be effective twice before. It was nothing unusual: threats, alternating with promises, and, above all, keeping them on their feet and awake. Uzi and I took turns, an hour each, while the other covered them with my old Beretta, a 1934 model I'd had for years. We kept them awake with cups of Arab coffee brewed over a kerosene stove that stank up the place, and when the coffee gave out, a couple of slaps across the face. Even so, just before dawn the older one, who was a lieutenant, fell asleep standing up.

Uzi slapped him, and all at once, without premeditation, because we weren't getting anywhere, we began beating them up. I hit the younger one in the corner of his mouth with my fist, and his eyetooth split the inside of his upper lip. We let him bleed. He was about twenty, a private, still in his khaki uniform, with the red-and-white checkered *kaffiah*, the headdress of the Legion, wrapped around his neck like a kerchief. His mouthful of blood embarrassed and scared the hell out of him. You could tell by the look in his eyes. He was afraid to spit it out and mess up the floor. Finally he took off the *kaffiah* and, crumpling it up in his hand, spit into that. Then he gagged and puked in it but, still terrified, stuffed it into the breast pocket of his tunic. His lip swelled up and made it hard for him to talk.

"I don't know," he kept repeating. "I swear I don't know. I have no idea."

The lieutenant, who had a swollen right cheek, never said a word or even made a sound. He was about thirty, and good-looking, with a deep cleft in his chin and a carefully clipped little mustache. The British officers who had trained him had done a good job. He was a professional soldier and proud of it. He stood at parade rest, in the middle of the room, with his hands clasped behind his back and his feet spread about a yard apart, according to regulations. That was the way he had fallen asleep.

"The kid," Uzi whispered to me. "Our only chance is the kid."

He punched him in the stomach, and the boy doubled up and fell, knocking over a small table with his shoulder. The coffee cups and a half bottle of brandy shattered on the tile floor.

All of a sudden, there was a pounding on the door that grew louder and wouldn't stop until I opened it a crack to catch a glimpse of the old man. There were phylacteries bound to his forehead. We had interrupted his morning prayers.

"What is it? What's happening here?" he asked me in Yiddish.

"Go away," I told him. "It's none of your business."

I tried to shut the door in his face, but he had already put one foot over the threshold, and with surprising strength threw the door wide open, looked around the room very slowly, and at me again, or rather, at the Beretta in my hand.

"Who is it?" Uzi asked. "What's he want?"

"Rosenblum," I told him. "From across the hall."

"Well, get him out of here."

The boy was still on the floor, gasping for breath, but he managed to raise himself up on his elbows to stare at the old man.

"Go on, now, beat it," Uzi told him in Hebrew.

"No," he answered in Yiddish, and he shook his head. His long earlocks waved. He understood Hebrew perfectly, of course, but as a Hassid he refused to use the holy tongue in ordinary conversation.

"Get him out of here," Uzi repeated. In the distance, maybe three or four blocks away, up Ben Yehuda Street, there was an explosion. The windows rattled. The Arabs were shelling us from the Old City. As a matter of fact, when I look back on it now, they had been shelling and mortaring us all night long, at irregular intervals. We were just impervious to it; only our bodies reacted instinctively every time there was an explosion. Everyone—even the lieutenant, I noticed with satisfaction—contracted his shoulders and ducked his head. Once, about seven in the morning, when an ambulance clanged up Jaffa Road in the direction of the King David, I went to the window to take a look. The street was strewn with rubble: broken glass, glittering in the fresh light, rolls of toilet paper, the burned-out wreck of an old Packard sedan, and fragments of the beautiful, rose-colored stone, quarried from the Judean hills, from which the houses of the New City are built.

The old man had apparently completed his prayers. He unwrapped his phylacteries from his forehead —the black felt hat was pushed far back on the crown of his head—and from his thin right arm, covered with red hair.

"You were born here?" he asked Uzi.

"What of it?"

"Were you?"

"Yes, in Haifa, where I live. So what?"

"And you, if I remember, in Tel Aviv," the old man said to me.

"Yes."

He slammed the door shut behind him with his foot and stood there, with his head raised and arms folded across his chest. It was a stance that in some way resembled the lieutenant's, communicating a determination not to give in, but in his case—the old man's—to speak.

"Haifa and Tel Aviv," he repeated. "No, then you mustn't."

Uzi tapped his temple with his forefinger. The old man saw it and smiled. "You think so? 'Have I need of madmen, that ye have brought this fellow to play the madman in my presence?' " He quoted the Bible in Hebrew. I had to think a moment and then remembered. It was from Samuel, when David had feigned insanity to escape from the king of Gath. "You have need," the old man whispered in Yiddish. "You have need. Let them go."

Maybe, from the tone of his voice, the boy guessed what the old man intended; anyhow, he smiled, or tried to smile, with his swollen lip. The lieutenant yawned, delicately covering his mouth with his hand.

Then the old man was off again, spouting from Isaiah, in a hoarse, singsong voice. " 'No lion shall be there, nor any ravenous beast shall go up thereon, it will not be found there; but the redeemed shall walk there.' "

He cleared his throat. His voice was hoarse, and for the first time I noticed his bulbous nose was red. He had a summer cold.

"Let them go," he said.

Uzi dragged the boy to his feet by the collar and hit him in the stomach again. He gagged but didn't have anything else to bring up.

"Well?"

Held at arm's length, his knees sagging, the boy shook his head. Uzi hit him again and let him drop to the floor, where he rolled over on his back.

"Listen to me," the old man said. "You must listen to me."

For the next ten minutes or so, Uzi and I took turns beating the boy up while the lieutenant and the old man watched. I concentrated on his mouth, and that eyetooth finally came out.

"Don't know," he mumbled. "Don't know."

It was possible that he was telling the truth, but we had less than an hour left, and we had to make sure. Uzi hit him in the stomach once more, and then we both had the same idea at the same time. All I had done was unconsciously scratch the nape of my neck with the muzzle of the Beretta. The lieutenant, who was yawning again, lowered his hand, took a deep breath, and straightened up. He understood too.

"Shoot him," Uzi said in Arabic. The boy, on the floor, opened his eyes.

I made a big production out of it, unloading the

magazine, counting the rounds—there were four .380 Colt cartridges—and reinserting it into the handle until it locked with a click. Then I drew back the slide, let it drive the bullet into the firing chamber, closed it, and released the safety. Except for his swollen cheek, which had turned purple, the lieutenant was as white as a sheet, but hadn't moved a muscle. I raised the gun and took aim between his eyes, but the old man grabbed it by the barrel, and I was so surprised, I let go. The lieutenant jumped to one side, to the right, toward the window, but it didn't do him any good. He was off balance, on his right knee, with his right hand on the floor, when the first round hit him in the chest, throwing him on his back. The old man walked over to him and emptied the rest of the magazine into his forehead, holding the gun a yard from his face.

"*Ai, Yah Allah,*" the boy screamed, "Oh, God," and, wringing his hands, began to talk so fast that Uzi, who was scribbling all the information down on a pad of yellow paper, made him slow down and repeat himself again and again. He told us everything we wanted to know, but I wasn't listening. I was looking at the old man, who gingerly handed me back the gun, holding it by the barrel, his little finger in the air. Then he sneezed. Before I could stop him, he walked out the door, across the hall, and into his apartment.

A week later, I was temporarily transferred to G.H.Q. in Tel Aviv to help correlate Intelligence for Operation Ten Plagues that eventually destroyed the Egyptian expeditionary force in the Negev. When I finally got back to Jerusalem, the war had been over for a month. I occasionally ran into the old man on the stairs, but we never spoke. He was usually on his way to shul, or coming back, and, still deeply absorbed in his prayers, looked right through me. His eyes were blue and slightly glazed with the madness that had made him take my crime upon himself because I had been born in the country into which his God had returned the Jews to give them their last chance.

Charity

MY MOTHER DIED IN THE WINTER OF 1912 when I was twelve years old. At the time, I was living with my parents in one room of a cold-water flat on Ludlow Street on Manhattan's Lower East Side. My father was a finisher of men's pants. He lined the pants at the waistline and hemmed the pockets. Working twelve hours a day on his rented Singer sewing machine, he made an average of seven dollars a week. While I went to school, my mother helped him by sewing on buttons and buckles. After school, my job was to deliver bundles of the finished pants to the subcontractor on Stanton Street who had hired us.

All told, we cleared a little over ten dollars a week. We paid fourteen dollars a month rent and ate very little: a roll and a cup of chicory-flavored coffee for breakfast, a bowl of chicken soup for lunch, and a crust of rye bread and big green pickles for supper. I always went to bed hungry. The only time we splurged on food was on Friday nights in celebration of the coming of the Sabbath. As a religious Jew, my father insisted upon it. We scrimped and saved all week and on Friday afternoons my mother went shopping on Hester Street, where she bought everything from the pushcart peddlers or the outdoor stalls. Beginning Friday morning, my mouth would actually water in anticipation.

When I got home, the table—the only one we owned—would already be set with a pair of brass candlesticks and chipped china plates with little rosebuds painted on them. There would be a fresh loaf of challah, covered by a threadbare embroidered doily, a little glass goblet of sweet red wine for each of us, a plate of stuffed carp, sweet-and-sour meat, roast potatoes saturated with gravy, and candied carrots. Soup—chicken soup again—made from legs and wings, always came last, and for dessert my mother would serve calf's-foot jelly which she had cooked that afternoon and set out on the fire escape to cool. Mother would light the candles, pronounce the benediction over them, and after blessing the bread and wine, my father would turn to our guest with a nod and invite him to begin eating.

We always had a guest on Friday nights, someone even poorer than we, and alone, who had no place to go to celebrate the Sabbath. It was a religious obligation my father had brought with him from Russia. On Friday afternoons, he would take an hour off from work to wander the streets of the neighborhood, looking for a Jewish beggar or a starving Hebrew scholar who slept on the benches of some shul. They were almost always old men smelling of snuff, who wore ragged beards, earlocks, and had dirty fingernails.

They would wash their hands in the sink, mumble their prayers, and, smacking their wrinkled lips, begin to eat, making grunting noises deep in their throats. Very often, on particularly cold nights, my father would invite them to remain with us, and they would curl up on the table, covered by a woolen blanket. Their snoring made it impossible for me to sleep.

"Papa," I'd complain.

"Shhh!" he'd tell me. "Remember. 'Charity saves from death.' "

He quoted the words from the Bible in Hebrew in a resonant voice that never failed to shut me up. I would lie awake in the dark, listening to the mingled sounds of the snoring, the wheezing and occasional cough, along with the scurrying of mice across the floor. The room was freezing. Coal was too expensive to keep the stove burning all night. Very often, in the mornings, the glass of water by my bed would be frozen solid.

Then, quite suddenly, in the middle of December, my mother caught pneumonia. She awoke on a Wednesday, as I remember, about midnight, with a splitting headache and a severe chill that made her teeth chatter and a raging fever that for some reason flushed only the left side of her face. It looked as if she had been slapped. Every bone in her body ached, she complained, and within a few hours, at about two in the morning, she was suffering from an agonizing pain in her right side.

"Like a knife," she whispered through clenched teeth.

Convulsed by a short, dry cough, she lay in bed for two more days. The left side of her face was still flushed. She breathed very quickly, with a grunt every time she exhaled. When she drew a breath, her nostrils were distended. There were open sores on her upper lip. Her dark brown eyes were peculiarly bright —I had never seen them so beautiful. I wanted to kiss the quivering lips. But the barking cough made her

raise herself up and claw at her right side. She began
to spit blood.

In her semi-delirium, she babbled half-remembered
legends from her childhood, and things she had read
in Yiddish chapbooks written for women.

"Is it snowing?" she asked me.

"Yes."

"Ah, but not there," she whispered. "Never there."

"Where?" my father asked her, and she gazed at
him with her glittering eyes, and smiled. "Where do
you think? Where there are fruit trees, trees with
golden leaves, always in bloom. Apple trees and
orange trees, and one huge tree, they say, where
apples, oranges, pears, and grapes grow on the same
branches, all together . . ."

He rubbed her moist, hot hands. "Listen to me.
This kind of talk is forbidden. Forbidden, Malka, do
you understand me? Can you hear me? It's absolutely
forbidden to talk this way. One must want to live."

"I've been a good wife, haven't I?" she asked.

"Of course."

"I've tried. God knows, I've tried to be a good wife,
a good mother, and a good Jew."

"Of course you have," my father said.

"I'm glad. I've read, you know, that when a right-
eous soul is about to enter Paradise, the angels come

and strip off her shroud and dress her in seven robes woven from the clouds of glory. Did you know that? Seven shining robes. And on her head they put two crowns. One of gold and the other . . . I forget now what the other is . . ."

"Stop it!" my father yelled.

"I remember," she said. "Pearls. A crown of pearls . . ."

When I came home that Friday afternoon, a doctor was there from the hospital on Second Avenue and Seventeenth Street. He was a tall German Jew who wore a blond goatee.

"Yes," he said in English, putting away his stethoscope. "The crisis will come in a week, maybe a little less."

"The crisis?" I repeated. "What's that?"

And looking down at me, he stroked his goatee. "A crisis is a crisis, my boy. It's as simple as that. She'll continue to get worse until the crisis, and then, if she's strong enough, her fever will drop and she'll survive. Of course, she'd have a much better chance in the hospital."

"What's that?" my father asked in Yiddish. "What's he saying?"

"It's up to you," the doctor went on, addressing me.

"But that's my considered professional opinion."

"A hospital?" my father suddenly repeated in English. It was probably the only word he had understood. He shook his head. "No . . ." His eyes filled with tears. I knew what he was thinking. In the shtetl north of Odessa from which he'd come, the hospital was a shack on the edge of town, supported by the local burial society, where the poor were sent to die.

My mother coughed, the doctor glanced at the face of a gold watch he wore suspended from a gold chain on his vest, and said, "Well?"

"This is America, Papa," I told him. "The doctor says that Mama will have a much better chance in the hospital."

The watch ticked, my mother gasped for breath, and my father finally nodded his head.

"Good," the doctor said. "I'll make the arrangements. The ambulance will be here in about an hour. In the meantime, keep her as warm as possible."

And when I had wrapped my mother in my own quilt, stuffed with goose feathers, my father said, "God forgive me. I almost forgot."

"What?"

"You'll have to do the shopping," he told me.

"For what?"

"For the Sabbath, what do you think?"

"Tonight?"

"The Sabbath is the Sabbath."

"I'm not hungry tonight."

"But our guest will be."

"Tonight?" I repeated.

"And why should tonight be different from last Friday night, or the Friday before that?"

My mother coughed again into her handkerchief. When she brought it away from her mouth, it was soaked with blood.

"Listen to your father," she whispered.

"No."

"Do what he tells you," she said.

I went down to Hester Street. In spite of the bitter cold and the grimy slush in which the horse-drawn wagons had made ruts, it was jammed with shoppers. For a moment, I stopped in front of a pushcart peddler who was selling cracked eggs at a penny apiece. Then, all at once, I understood. It was a *mitzvah* my father was performing, a good deed, a holy act, which bound together the upper and nether worlds, and hastened the redemption of Israel. I glanced up at the low clouds, hanging just above the city, which had a reddish glow, reflecting the lights below. It was a sign; the heavens and the earth had come closer together. And tonight of all nights, when it was a matter of life and death. The Holy One, blessed be He, saw everything. My father's charity would not go un-rewarded. I walked on through the slush that seeped into my shoes. Scrawny chickens and half-plucked geese hung by their feet in a doorway and, still flutter-ing, awaited the butcher's knife. The butcher himself, his brawny arms covered with feathers and spattered with blood, chewed on a black cigar, spat into the gutter, and tested the blade of his knife on the ball of his thumb. It began to snow.

By the time I reached home, my mother was gone, but there with my father was a tall, emaciated, stoop-shouldered man wearing a ragged black frock coat and a battered black silk top hat. Over one arm, he carried an umbrella.

"This is Reb Rifkin," said my father.

"I know. *Shabbat shalom.*"

"And a peaceful Sabbath to you, too," Rifkin an-swered me in his high, cracked voice.

I had seen him around the neighborhood for years. He was a broken-down Hebrew teacher who barely kept himself alive by giving Hebrew lessons for ten cents apiece. He lived in a shul on Essex Street, where he slept in a tiny unheated room behind the Ark. It was said that rats had once attacked him and bitten off part of one of his toes.

Shivering, he warmed his blue hands over the coal stove while my father and I prepared supper. Because the doctor had been so expensive—two dollars—we had only a little chicken soup with noodles, half a loaf of stale challah, the head of a carp, a bowlful of raisins and almonds for dessert, and a glass of steaming tea with lemon. My father gave Rifkin the fish head and he devoured everything except the eyes and the bones, which he sucked one by one.

"God bless you," he said, wiping his fingers on his beard. "Would you believe it? Except for a little salted herring and a glass of tea, this is the only thing I've had in my mouth for six days. As God is my witness. Six whole days."

A little color had already seeped into his thin face with its greenish complexion. He had a tiny white spot on his right pupil which made him seem unable to look you straight in the eye. He appeared to gaze slightly above you and a little to the left.

"How's Mama?" I asked my father.

"In God's hands."

"How true. Aren't we all?" asked Rifkin. "If I hadn't gone for a walk on Ludlow Street and met you, I'd be in my room right now, lying in the dark. Do you know that the rats there eat my candles?"

"When can we visit her?" I went on.

"Tomorrow."

"I heard the sad news," Rifkin said to me. "But don't you worry about a thing. God willing, she'll be well in no time."

"I hope so," my father said.

"How can you doubt it?" Rifkin cried out. "God is just, but He's merciful too. To whom will He not show His mercy if not to a fine woman like that and her husband who feeds the starving?"

"We shall see," my father said.

"Well, I should be going," said Rifkin, picking up his umbrella.

"Nonsense," my father said. "It's snowing. You'll stay the night and share breakfast with us tomorrow morning. Lunch and supper too, if you like. Whatever we have in the house."

"No, no, I couldn't think of it."

"But I insist."

"Well, of course, if you put it like that . . ."

As I had expected, Rifkin snored; not only snored, but whistled. I couldn't sleep, so I got up and with the blanket wrapped around my shoulders went out onto the landing. We lived on the fourth floor. The building reeked of urine from the toilets at the end of each

hallway and the smell of cooked cabbage, fried on-
ions, and fish. There was the whir of sewing ma-
chines. To make ends meet, God help us, some Jews
were forced to work on the Sabbath. I sat down on the
steps. The words of the proverb rang in my head:
". . . but he that hath mercy on the poor, happy is he."

"Jacob, is that you?" my father whispered when I
went back into the room.

"Yes, Papa."

"Are you all right?"

"Fine, Papa."

"Come over here a minute."

"What's the matter?"

"I can't sleep."

"Neither could I, but I feel much better now."

"Do you? Why?"

"Because Mama will get well."

"How can you be so sure?"

"You said so yourself."

"Did I? When?"

"You said that charity saves from death."

"What's that got to do with Mama?"

"Everything."

He suddenly raised his voice. "Is that what you
think a *mitzvah* is? A bribe offered the Almighty?"

"But you said so. You said that charity saves from

death," I insisted. Rifkin, half awakened, turned over and groaned.

"No, not Mama," my father said in a hoarse voice. "Him."

Grace

AND THEN YOU DIED?"

"Oh, yes," she said. "It was quite simple. A sudden cessation of that terrible pain, and then the separation, rather like drawing a silk handkerchief from your pocket, or a hair from a glass of milk."

"As easy as all that?"

"As easy as that."

Turnbull waited for his aunt to go on. Up to now, up to a few minutes ago, when she had begun talking about her own heart attack four years ago, he thought that the old girl was taking her husband's death pretty well. She had arranged for the cremation herself, and at the memorial Meeting had sat in the front pew, pale but dry-eyed, while Thomas Oates, who had worked with Uncle Martin for forty years, testified:

". . . not only an eminent banker but a loving husband, and a man of great spiritual gifts, as well. A Friend, in the most profound sense of that word. Descended on his mother's side from William Salt, who with George Fox established, with the grace of God, the first Meeting in Cornwall, England, he not only . . ."

Sipping his sherry, Turnbull thought now, quite suddenly, that his aunt had been smiling through the whole service, beginning with Miss Pendleton, who had been the first to speak. She had worked with Uncle Martin as a recording clerk, a secretary, when he had been appointed head of the finance committee of the Yearly Meeting. She had a bad cold, and spoke in a barely audible, husky voice.

"It was Francis Howgill, one of our English martyrs, who died in prison in the seventeenth century . . ." Convulsed by one sneeze, and then another, she wiped her wet nose with a wad of Kleenex. "Yes," she went on. "Another Friend tried to comfort him, 'After all, Friend, what does it amount to? Merely moving from one room to another in the same house.' 'No, Friend,' said Howgill. 'From one corner to another, in the same room.' "

She sat down again, abruptly, blowing her nose.

And Turnbull's aunt had smiled. Not condescendingly; not her Lady Bountiful smile. He knew that well enough. Or what, over the years, he had called her Smile of the Suffering Servant. For fifteen years the old woman had an Irish downstairs maid, who had broken, in her time, a Czech crystal vase and a Royal Doulton shepherdess on the mantelpiece. Turnbull had seen the shepherdess go. A swipe of the dust rag, the maid's stricken face, and the shattering of the porcelain on the brass andiron. And then, of course, his aunt's smile, accompanied, for a moment, by lowered eyelids. The maid had retched and run through the dining room into the kitchen. And his aunt had said, "That girl has ruined my lunch."

Miss Pendleton sneezed again, and Turnbull's aunt kept smiling. But why? Because of Pendleton's sharp red nose with the wet nostrils, the watery eyes, and the dark hairs on her upper lip? Although in her late sixties, Turnbull's aunt was still a remarkably beautiful woman and proud of it.

His mother had suffered from the comparison all her life. Not that she ever said a word. But once, as a child of eight, Turnbull had overheard the women talking at home in Haverford, had heard his aunt's smile articulated as she said to her sister, "Sarah, there are things thee can do with your hair." Through the crack in the pantry door, Turnbull had suddenly

understood that his aunt ascribed a kind of moral der-
eliction to the plain or homely, as though they were
that way by choice and could change by rectitude or
discipline. As if his mother's thinning chestnut hair
could become fuller or lustrous, or Miss Pendleton's
mustache disappear.

But sipping his sherry, across from his aunt seated
on the blue sofa, Turnbull realized that it hadn't been
any of those at all. It had been a smile of acknowl-
edgment.

She was smiling now, recollecting, as she twirled
the stem of her glass between her fingers.

"Then I stood up," she said. "And I looked around.
Martin was kneeling down, on one knee, and I put my
hand on his shoulder, to let him know that everything
was all right. But the oddest thing. My hand—it was
my left, with my wedding ring, which I could clearly
see—went right through him. 'Now, that's very odd,'
I thought. 'Very odd, indeed.' But before I could say
anything, I saw the woman, lying on the sidewalk at
his feet. She looked dreadful. Pale, dreadfully pale,
a kind of ashen gray, shiny from perspiration.

"Her eyes were closed. 'That woman is dead,' I
thought. I was about to speak to Martin, when I noticed that she was wearing a Persian-lamb coat. Mine.

There was no mistaking it. It was too long, and I had meant to have it shortened. And then I saw my patent-leather handbag and the shoes to match. She was clutching the bag in her left hand. I took a closer look at her face. It was me, but for some reason, in spite of the pallor, looking younger. Ten years younger, maybe more. No wrinkled lips or crow's-feet.

"I straightened up and rose in the air four or five feet, effortlessly, and just hung there, as in one of those delightful dreams in which we're able to fly. Only the air was as dense as water, and in order to remain steady, I had to balance myself—I don't know how. I'm a terrible swimmer. By an effort of the will.

"In any case, I looked down and could see the top of Martin's bald head, with its liver spots. And then I became aware that the body lying there, at his feet, was illuminated, bathed in a milky, transparent light, which seemed to be coming from behind me. I rose a little higher and to the left, above a fire hydrant, and the light shifted too. It reminded me of a ray of light from a movie projector. A cone of light. I thought it was a ray of sunlight, but it wasn't that at all. The sky was completely clouded over. It looked as if it were about to snow. Then I realized that the light was coming from me. As a matter of fact, my whole body was glowing faintly, although I cast no shadow, nor lit up anything else."

"The Inner Light," said Turnbull. "Obviously."

"Thee is joking, of course," she said, in her most frigid voice, with the Suffering Servant smile.

But then the voice thawed, and the smile was gone.

"No," she said softly. "That wasn't it at all. Although, in some way, I don't know how, the lights were related, and meant to merge. Mine, and the other, by which everything, all things, visible and invisible, are seen, thee see, by . . . Not that I saw the other. Oh, no. But I knew it was there, and that merging with it, in a manner I could only guess, was the reason for which I had been created.

"Then Martin began to hiccup. Terrible hiccups, as the tears streamed down his face. He got them often. Once for twenty-four hours. The doctor had to give him—I forget what. And I thought of his prostate trouble, his allergy to cats which made him break out in red blotches, his terror of getting cancer . . ."

"Not that it did him much good," Turnbull interrupted.

"No, poor dear. He was a terrible coward. When he found out he had it, he went to pieces for a month. That's when I took him to Palm Springs."

"I remember."

"Yes, and there was his inability to fall asleep, after thirty-eight years of marriage, unless I was in the double bed beside him."

She paused, absorbed in thought, and then went on. "How could I have left him alone? Even if I knew I was going to be liberated from the flesh, and changed, transformed so radically into . . . It's no use. I can only remember the intimation of that joy, which I so craved. But even that memory, day by day, hour by hour, even now, as we're chatting, is fading away, becoming, more and more, words, mere words . . . Yet all I had to do was let myself go, so to speak, and the light which bound me to that body would unravel like a length of yarn. But how could I?"

"How were you dressed?" Turnbull asked her.

"In my Persian coat and black patent-leather shoes."

"No, I mean in the spirit."

"In my Persian coat and black patent-leather shoes."

"How do you explain that?" he asked.

"I'm not sure," she said. "I think that immediately after death the habits of this life persist. We're habituated to thinking of ourselves as a body and this somehow perpetuates, at least temporarily, the illu-

73

sion of the body to which we're accustomed. But only
for a little while. Just before Martin hiccupped, something else was beginning to happen. Just for an instant, and only an intimation, mind thee, which, for
the life of me, I can't actually recall, but . . ."

She stopped again, her eyes shining with tears.

Turnbull was astonished; he had never seen this
before, even at the funeral of her father, to whom she
was fanatically devoted.

"More sherry?" she asked him.

"No, thank you."

"Poor Martin. Those dreadful hiccups. When the
intern from the hospital, from Lenox Hill, arrived
with the ambulance, Martin couldn't answer a single
question. But not one word! While the tears rolled
down his cheeks, I laughed. That's when I came
back."

"How?"

"I think . . . I concentrated. I thought to myself, if
I could just close that hand, or only flex the fingers a
little, just the forefinger, I could do it. And I did. I
tried, with all my will, and managed it. The finger
moved, and there I was, in frightful pain, from my
angina. In the chest, the heart, the left shoulder, and
all the way down the left arm. Even my jaw, and the

scalp, if thee can believe it, under the ear and above it, on the left side."

"Before or after the intern treated you?"

"Before."

"Are you sure?"

"Positive. Before, definitely. I'm sure of it."

"I see."

"The pain was simply frightful, but it wasn't that I minded at all, but the sense of loss. That . . . inkling of what I had lost by coming back, if thee understand what I mean."

"No, I'm afraid I don't."

"Ah well," she said. "Thee will see for thyself."

"Will I?" he asked her.

He left her apartment at ten, intending to go immediately back to the office. The closing of Miles's private placement was tomorrow at three, and Turnbull still had a lot of work to do on it. He walked down Park, looking for a cab, and found himself in front of a huge Catholic church. An empty cab passed, heading downtown, but for some reason he turned instead and went up the steps, through a bronze door, and into a musty vestibule. To his left, a marble font, with a glass dish of holy water inside that reminded him of a soup plate. More steps, a double door, and he was inside.

The place was enormous, absolutely enormous, and empty. His footfall echoed on the floor as he looked around. A double row of massive, red, highly polished granite columns, with Corinthian capitals, led, on either side of the wide aisle, to the main altar. The façade was sixteenth-century Italian Renaissance, and well done. But the interior was in the Roman style. A Roman temple—or almost. And there, to his right, an idol: a marble Virgin, holding the Child in her left arm, set within a shallow apse. Then he saw the Baptistry. It was hideous, surrounded by an ornate wrought-iron fence, above which was the large mosaic portraying the Baptism of Christ.

Actually, Turnbull realized, it was a painting which imitated a mosaic. The two figures had been rendered by innumerable distinct little squares which made their flesh appear to be covered by scales, like reptiles. Suspended above Jesus' head, John's right hand, with its particularly long, bent fingers, looked like a lizard's claw.

Turnbull looked up at the white dove, and realized why he had come. Surrounded by a semicircular gilt —mandorla? nimbus? halo? Turnbull couldn't remember the right term—it had been pictured from above, with the wings extended, and the tail feathers spread, rather like a fan. It had a scarlet beak.

He recalled the words of Luke: "And the Holy Ghost descended in a bodily shape like a dove . . ." He had read somewhere that the dove was a vicious bird, which attacked its own kind for no particular reason, going for the eyes with that scarlet beak. What of it? It was what the Holy Spirit had once chosen to become; a mob, wading in a river, had seen It—a mob. He grasped the iron bars and pressed his forehead between them.

In his office, he read: "Although the opinion in Columbia Steel illuminated the prior precedents, the decision upholding the absorption of an industrial giant was so disappointing . . ." He snapped the book shut and said aloud, "Preposterous!"

Two or three years ago, he had read an article in *The Saturday Evening Post* about an accountant who had suffered anaphylactic shock from a bee bite. In Scarsdale. Turnbull recalled it all vividly. The man had been bitten on his left arm, in his rose garden in Scarsdale, and had suffered an acute allergic reaction which, in a few minutes, had killed him. He was dead. Clinically dead: no pulse, no blood pressure, no heartbeat. The eyes, like Uncle Martin's, glazed, the flesh ashen, the limbs flaccid. Dead. He had been resuscitated by his family doctor, a next-door neighbor who had known of the accountant's allergy. The doctor had immediately given the man intravenous injections of antihistamines, as Turnbull recalled, and a massive dose of adrenalin.

But the man had been dead for almost a minute and, when resuscitated, had remembered nothing of what it had been like. He had been aware of his swollen lips, which itched and then became numb in the instant before death. But afterward, nothing, a void, until he began coming around and felt and heard the thunderous pounding of his own heart—the adrenalin—and saw a blur of color to his right, his wife's red dress. But, in between, nothing.

" 'I remembered nothing.' "

Turnbull had read the article five or six times and repeated the man's words aloud. "Nothing," he said.

The sound of his own voice startled him. He had spoken softly. No one could have heard, but the sound had made him intensely aware of the silence in the room. It was in some way constricted by the rows of leather-bound books on the shelves, the thick rug, and the red velvet draperies drawn across the windows. He had always preferred to work by artificial light, a brass lamp with a leather shade on his leather-topped walnut desk—he had a passion for the smell of leather and wood—but now the odors nauseated him. He was suffocating, stood up, undid the top button of his shirt, and loosened his tie. No better. He gasped for breath. It wasn't the smells, but the silence. He remembered with relief that expansive silence of the Catholic church—his echoing footfall on the marble floor. And then the small noises at Meeting that morning, before Miss Pendleton had gotten up to testify: the shuffle of feet, the creak of the wooden pews—only the backs, the seats were cushioned in red plush—somebody clearing his throat and, then again, half gagging, bringing up a mouthful of phlegm.

Turnbull was reminded of a fragment from the *Journal* of George Fox, which he had memorized, and which had anguished him as a child: "And Your growth is the Seed in the Silence, / Where ye may all find a Feeding of the Bread of Life." He had believed for years that the suffocating silence of his office just now, somehow internalized, was what he had to achieve so that, hollowed out, he would be filled.

Once, only once, when he was thirteen, in early June, something had happened at Meeting. It was a gray, overcast day, and drizzling. The raindrops ran down the window to his left, and looking outside, thinking of nothing in particular, he noticed that a rosebush, near a maple tree, had bloomed since last Sunday. They were ordinary tea roses, American Beauties, like the ones his mother grew in the front yard of their house on Panmure Road. A gust of wind, the raindrops splatted against the windows, and the roses swayed.

"They're alive," he thought. "Alive, and at the same time, on fire, and holy. Burning . . .

"*Burning . . . a rose's fire burning smokeless in a summer rain.*"

He was flabbergasted. It was the first, and the only, line of poetry he had ever composed—if that's what it was. He would have to ask his father. He glanced at him seated on his right. Then he looked out of the window again. The rain was coming down much harder; the trunk of the maple tree was black, and he couldn't see the rosebush.

Years later, at a cocktail party on East Sixty-fourth Street, he chatted with a fashion photographer, who explained the extraordinary radiance of the roses.

"My dear, there's no mystery about it at all. . . . An overcast day, you say. Well, there you have it. Sunlight, you see, would have burned out the color of the roses, but the diffused gray light emphasized them.

Heaven knows, it's a common enough situation, working outdoors. An ultraviolet filter, and you're all set. It's as simple as that."

But Turnbull remained puzzled by something else: the rapture he had experienced. Like pain, the sensation was impossible to recall, and now, muddled by three Martinis, he couldn't think what had caused it. It was only after another drink, leaning his elbows on the coffee table between his empty glass and a dish of salted almonds, that the reason came to mind: he had realized that the moment in which those roses had existed was eternal. No, that wasn't it. He chewed an almond. It was the other way around. Eternity—all eternity—had existed in that moment when the wind swayed the roses with their dark, glossy leaves, and that realization had filled him with ecstasy.

For almost a year afterward, the Experience, as he came to call it, had given him some small hope. Perhaps, after all, he had some small spiritual gift, a minor talent for loving God, or at least what God had created.

His mother had it. At Meeting, she never spoke up. She sat with her eyes closed and her hands folded in her lap. And then, one December morning, just before the end of service, she stood up and suddenly recited a portion from the Psalm: " 'For Thee my flesh and my heart hath fainted away . . .' "

At first, her husky, trembling voice made the boy think she had been embarrassed. She always spoke in a high, clear, firm tone. Yes, that was it: acute embarrassment. Her drawn face was flushed, and her hands shook as she folded them again in her lap.

But an hour later at lunch, her hand was still shaking as she pricked the veal roast with a fork and the clear yellow juice oozed out.

"Is it done?" Turnbull's father asked. "I'm starving."

She nodded, and catching her eye, the boy realized that she was still afraid to trust her voice. She wasn't embarrassed. He stared at her across a plate of baked potatoes. Her face was unrecognizable; it was a face he had never seen before, with those flushed cheeks, dilated nostrils, and luminous hazel eyes.

"It's absolutely marvelous," Turnbull's father said. "What's the matter with you two? You haven't touched a bite."

"I'm not hungry," the boy said, and excusing himself, he ran upstairs and locked himself in his room. Under the papers scattered on his desk—the draft of a five-hundred-word essay on the significance of the porter in *Macbeth*—was a Bible. He turned to the

Psalm, and began to read aloud, " 'For Thee my flesh and my heart . . .' "

Then he began leafing through the New Testament, but it was useless, and he knew it: there was no physical description of Jesus anywhere—neither His height, the color of His hair, His eyes, or the shape of His mouth. Yet He had been a man: his mother must have imagined some man who had been able to evoke that husky voice, those flushed cheeks, dilated nostrils, and luminous eyes.

He dropped the book to the floor, went to the window, and looked down into the front yard. Almost a foot of snow had fallen during the night, and a north wind, blowing in gusts all day, had frozen the surface. The glazed crust glistened in the diminishing afternoon light.

The boy leaned his forehead against the icy pane and thought, "God forgive me. It's not true. It's not possible. Not Mama." And then, with tears gathering in his eyes, he remembered her contempt for a huge stained-glass window of Christ Enthroned in a Catholic church they'd once passed in Philadelphia.

"Just look at that! Idolatry, pure and simple!" And smiling, she had added, "To say nothing of the sheer audacity! Red hair and blue eyes! They've made Him look Irish!"

He picked up the Bible, sat down at his desk, and tried to pray, but it was useless. A single tear, rolling down his right cheek, fell on one of the sheets of paper before him, smudging the ink of the *u* in the word "circumstances," which, for some forgotten reason, he had underlined twice.

The essay got a B: the lowest grade he received for a paper in English all year. It was far and away his best subject, and he prided himself on his ability to write clearly. He never spoke to his father, though, about the line of poetry he had made up. It seemed so amateurish.

The old man, who died in 1963 at the age of seventy-four, had taught seventeenth-century English poetry at Haverford, specializing in George Herbert, for whom he had a passion. The boy, too, adored the poet, envied him his faith, but was terrified by his lines:

> When boyes go first to bed,
> They step into their voluntarie graves.

His mother, while disapproving, had allowed him a night-light until he was thirteen. On the night of his fourteenth birthday, his father, who had given him a splendid pair of hiking shoes, ordered especially from a firm in Maine, kissed him on the forehead and turned off the light.

His room, with its dresser, the walls, even the walnut headboard of his bed, was suddenly obliterated. The darkness seemed to be not merely the absence of light but something palpable and corrosive that was dissolving his body, annihilating it. Only the indomitable beating of his heart, the pounding in his chest, prevented him from screaming. And then, as his eyes became gradually accustomed to the darkness, he began to see dim, familiar shapes: the linen curtain on his window, stirring in a breeze, the headboard, the dresser, and his right hand. Soaked with sweat, tossing and turning in his bed, he was unable to fall asleep until dawn.

After that, for almost a year, he took the hiking shoes to bed with him, and stroked the cowhide and thick rubber soles and heels until his eyes got used to the dark. The heavy shoes in his invisible hands reassured him. He and the shoes, after all, were made of atoms—the same, fundamental matter. Leather, rubber, flesh: when you got right down to it, what was the basic difference between them? Or that headboard? It was impossible for the darkness to dissolve them. He always fell asleep on his back, with one shoe in each hand.

Yet he hated to go hiking in the woods with his father, who had a taste for broiled squirrel: ordinary red squirrels, with bright eyes, which in the spring he would catch in traps baited with horse chestnuts. The traps broke their backs, and he would bring them home, skin them in the garage with a hunting knife, and keep them in the refrigerator. The raw, headless little corpses, all curled up, with their pawless limbs reminded Turnbull of human fetuses, kept in flasks, he had once seen on a tour of the campus with his father. But when squirrel was served for dinner, saturated in Cumberland sauce, Turnbull would have to eat it. His father insisted on it.

"Try it," he said. "It's delicious. There's nothing reprehensible about killing game for food. How do you suppose the Friends who came to Pennsylvania with Penn—your own great-great-great-great-great-grandfather Jedediah provided meat for his family in the wilderness?"

The boy glanced at his mother, who averted her eyes. She never touched the squirrels herself, but as she always deferred to her husband, and had never once argued with him in front of the boy, she refused to interfere.

"Well, one has to eat," the boy thought to himself. "I love veal, and what about vegetables? There's no real difference between a rose and a cabbage, and I eat cabbages all the time. It's God's will that we have to kill living things in order to stay alive."

The broiled squirrels still nauseated him, but in silent prayer, at Meetings, he was comforted that eating the flesh was almost a sacred act. Since the purpose of human intelligence was to adore God, the death of life which sustained it was, in a way, transfigured: a holy sacrifice.

"Only answer me," he prayed, with tears in his eyes. "Just give me one more sign."

His father, sitting next to him, yawned behind his hand. He was one of the lukewarm, the boy finally decided, who attended Meeting only because it pleased his wife, and because he was proud of belonging to an old Quaker family distantly related to Rufus Jones.

But the boy knew that, with meditation and prayer, God would respond to everyone. George Fox, who had once been a cobbler, still wore leather breeches after he had become a preacher, to show that he remained a common man. He had used Plain Talk to everyone, because he had refused to distinguish between men of different classes. He had known that the Holy Spirit was accessible to them all.

On the night after the funeral, Turnbull had slight

indigestion. He took an Alka-Seltzer, belched twice, and got some relief. Now he was rereading an article in the *Harvard Law Review* for a brief he was preparing for early next month. "Rule X-16B2 exempts underwriting transactions where a person . . ."

He yawned, belched again, thumped his chest with his fist, and skipped down to the bottom of the paragraph. "The insider-underwriter and to an extent at least as equal to the aggregate participation of all persons exempted by the rule."

"Exempted . . ."

He put the magazine away, on the shelf in his night table, next to a thick volume bound in beige, *A Practical Guide to Oriental Rugs*. Six or seven years ago, he had become very interested in Oriental rugs. Now they bored him, but he occasionally leafed through the book as a soporific.

He turned out the light. On the twentieth floor— the reason he had bought this apartment—the reddish glow of the low clouds, reflecting the lights of the city, dimly illuminated his bedroom. In the mirror over his dresser, when he raised his head, he could see, within its depths, a faintly phosphorescent reflection of his clothes-closet door, on the opposite wall.

He closed his eyes, and suddenly opened them again and sat up.

He had been thinking of his mother, and the wonderful odor he associated with her—apple turnovers, cooling in her pantry. Then he had thought of Jesus, quoted in Romans, quoting Moses, quoting God: "I will have mercy on whom I will have mercy."

"It isn't fair," Turnbull said aloud. "It isn't fair."

In the Reign
of Peace

B Y THREE-THIRTY, WHEN WE FINISHED WORK IN the orchard, there was almost nothing left of the mouse: a blotch of dried blood on the flagstones, to which a little tuft of fur was still stuck. The bones, ground to powder, had been blown away by the wind. All the ants were gone. Chaim said nothing. It was Friday, and we had quit early so that he could return home to Kiriat Shemona before sundown to attend the service in the Moroccan synagogue there. And as always at the coming of the Sabbath, he solemnly shook my hand.

"*Shabbat shalom.*"

"Yes, and to you too," I told him. "A peaceful Sabbath."

With the eight other workers hired by the kibbutz,

he boarded the truck outside the communal dining hall. They were all recent North African or Iraqi immigrants; not yet so proficient in Hebrew, they jabbered away in Arabic, all excited by the anticipation of a good meal and a day of rest. Only Chaim, who secured the chain of the tail gate, remained silent. For a moment, squinting up at him in the sun, I had the impression that I was looking at him through the eyes of a goy, just as my grandfather must have been seen by the Poles in Kraków. And with the same hatred. The truck started up, the chain rattled, and Chaim waved. With the other hand, he held onto his hat. It was because of that hat he always wore—a battered green fedora, stained with sweat—his thick black beard, and his sidelocks which he tucked up above his ears—everything with which he set himself apart.

At seven, my wife and I put Ethan to bed in the Children's House. He's four, and wants to sleep with us in our room, but rules are rules.

"Shabbat shalom."

The greeting, exchanged in the twilight, by the kibbutz members, meant nothing. We would work tomorrow, like any other day—harder. The cows would be milked, the eggs collected, and we would begin picking the apples. It's the one thing about us that Chaim still refuses to believe.

"Jews working on the Sabbath? Ah, now you're joking with me," he once said.

"Haven't you?"

"No, thanks be to God."

"Never? Not even once in Rabat?"

"Never," he said, and in his guttural accent, which rasped in the back of his throat, he told me something about his life in Morocco.

The Sabbath had preserved him. It had been his only respite from the work that had earned him barely enough to keep himself and his family alive: carrying hundredweight sacks of charcoal through those narrow, reeking streets to the Arab ironmongers.

On the Sabbath, he remained in the shack near the old entrance to the ghetto, where he lived in one room with his wife and six kids. For the most part, he slept away the day on the earthen floor. Once in a while he would be awakened by a wailing child and rouse himself to eat the cold remains of the Sabbath feast from the night before: a lamb pilaf, in which the fat and the rice had congealed. He ate only with the fingers of his right hand, like an Arab, and his children would lick them clean, one by one. It was all their mother would allow. Today the meat, even the fat, she told them, was only for their father. What would happen to them all if, God forbid, their father lost his strength?

Chaim could never keep awake for long. The heat and the buzzing of the flies made him sleepy. He always tried to recite at least a portion of the Sabbath prayer before he passed out again. "Exalt ye the Lord our God . . ."

Impossible. He was never once able to finish it. He sank back on the pile of greasy rags he used as a pillow. Just before his eyes closed, he saw one of his naked kids, on all fours, sniffing at his right hand— Masouda, his youngest daughter, whom the others always pushed aside.

"And now?" I asked him.

"Ah, now, praise His Name, I can pray in the synagogue for as long as I like."

"And does Masouda get enough to eat?"

"She's dead. She died two years ago, when we all caught the spotted fever." He spat between his fingers to avert the evil eye. "My wife lost all her hair. All of it, even between her legs."

He told me very little about his life in this country. He had been here almost a year, living in Kiriat Shemona. I could imagine the rest: the three-room flat, provided by the government for a nominal rent, and everything else bought on credit—the television set on which he watched American movies, dubbed in Arabic, broadcast from Beirut, the refrigerator, the gas stove, maybe a coffee table with a Formica top, and even a bed.

He worked wherever he could: repairing the northern frontier road, or for some kibbutz, like ours, that was always short-handed. He had been with us for a week. Unlike other Moroccans we had hired over the years—petty-bourgeois tradesmen, or those who wanted to be—he wasn't ashamed of working with his hands. He enjoyed it and had an instinctive feeling for tools: the long-handled, two-handed shears with which I taught him to prune the excess branches from the apple trees.

"That's it," I told him. "Gently, so you don't tear the bark. And not too near the trunk."

"What's that?"

"That's very important. It's white paint with lead in it."

"What for?"

"You must always smear it on the wound to prevent fungus infection."

"Fungus?"

"A kind of disease."

"Ah . . ."

And then, after he watched me for a moment, "Does the tree feel any pain?"

"No."

"But it gets sick just like us?"

"Exactly."

"I see," he said, and he stared in astonishment at the Baldwin apple tree that shared our fate.

In the days that followed, he would shut his shears and stare in the same way, with an open mouth, at the whole world of which he was now a part: the rotting apples, scattered on the earth, that swarmed with bees; the pear trees in the south orchard, with their glossy, pointed leaves; a yellow butterfly; a mouse scurrying through the dry grass.

By the end of the second week, at the beginning of June, it was obvious that there was going to be a bumper crop, the best in over three years.

Chaim said, "Praise His Name, you'll be a rich man."

"No, not me. It belongs to the kibbutz."

"This orchard isn't yours?"

"Of course not. I thought you understood that."

"*Ai, habibi,* no, I didn't know." For the first time

between us, he had used the Arabic endearment, only for lovers and friends. And then he whispered, "Tell me. How much do they pay you?"

"Nothing. I don't need any money. The kibbutz gives me everything I need."

"Free?"

"In return for my work."

"I don't understand."

"It's very simple." But I was too hot, too tired, and too hungry to go on. It was one o'clock, time for lunch.

We walked up the flagstone path, between the azalea bushes and the lilacs, toward the dining hall. Under the eucalyptus trees, I tried again.

"We share everything equally here. Can you understand that?"

"Oh, yes," he said. "Why?"

"Because it's just."

"Just?" He pricked up his ears at the word. It was a word he finally seemed to understand. Not from personal experience—those sacks of charcoal, the famished child smelling his hand—but perhaps from his Bible. The half-forgotten phrases came back to me from my childhood. "The way of the just is as shining light." "The path of the just . . ."

He said dubiously, "Ah, yes . . ."

At the sink, in the dining hall, while he carefully washed his hands, he muttered the benediction under his breath. And at the table, with closed eyes, he prayed again over a mug of water, a tomato, and two thick slices of rye bread. It was the only food of ours he ever touched. Even our white cheese was suspect. A plate of beef liver and noodles, set before him, made him avert his face. He chewed the dry bread and looked mournfully about him at the tables crowded with sunburned men and stout women wearing shorts and heavy boots.

"No one here is kosher?" he asked me.

"No one."

"Not one of you believes in God?"

"Not one."

"Or in the Messiah?"

"No."

"You don't believe in the coming of the Messiah?"

With my mouth stuffed with noodles, I shook my head, and he stared at me, appalled.

I should have known. It wasn't just the Sabbath which had sustained him in Rabat—that lamb pilaf and the few extra hours of sleep—but that absurd hope. He must have believed in the same kind of things as my grandfather: that, at the End of Days, when the Messiah comes, he'll raise the dead and restore the sacred cruse of oil to the Temple, which he'll rebuild with a wave of his hand.

For the rest of the afternoon, as we laid plastic irrigation pipes between the pear trees in the south orchard, Chaim was silent. Then, at five, when we quit for the day, he asked me, "You don't believe in redemption?"

It was in the same voice as before, with the same tone of incredulity and sadness, but now hoarse from fatigue.

"Yes," I told him. "I suppose, in a way, that I do. I believe that one day everyone will live like this."

"Like what?"

"Sharing everything."

"Is that all?"

"What more would you want?"

He said nothing. The sweat streamed down his face. His damp beard, which clung to the contour of his jaw, revealed a receding chin. It was unexpected and gratifying, the suggestion of some hidden weakness—an inconstancy—bred in the man's very bones.

By the second week in July, the apples were ripe. On Wednesday afternoon I went into Kiriat Shemona to our cooperative cold-storage plant and arranged for the disposition of our crop. Beginning Saturday, for eight days, we would ship and store six tons a day. The entire work force of the kibbutz would be mobilized to pick the apples. Each member would be required to work an extra twenty-four hours in the orchard. We would be at it from 4 a.m. to 6 p.m. in that July heat. Even the kids over thirteen would have to lend a hand.

On Friday, at noon, I went into the co-op again and brought back the big GMC with the electric winch and the aluminum bins in which the apples are packed. Chaim was waiting for me outside the dining hall. He had been squatting on his heels in the shadow of the overhanging roof. Now he stood up.

"What is it?" I asked him. "What's the matter?"

"Come and see."

I followed him down the flagstone path toward the orchard. It was almost two, the hottest time of the day. A gust of wind, blowing across the lawn, brought with it the smell of dry manure.

"Quick," he called out, breaking into a run.

Under the eucalyptus trees, he suddenly stopped and squatted down again on his haunches, leaning forward with his hands between his knees.

"There," he said. "You see? And still alive."

It was a mouse, a field mouse, with a white underside, which had evidently come up through a hole in

the concrete between two flagstones and gotten stuck
halfway. The forepaws waved in the air.

"What about it?"

"Look closer."

I knelt down beside him. The forepaws waved and
the head jerked up and down. I could see a black ant,
its antennae waving, in the right nostril. The mouse
was covered with ants, hundreds of them, that
swarmed over that palpitating white chest, the coarse,
tawny fur between the eyes, and in the large ears
bristling with short hairs. The ears were oozing blood.
A bright drop, flung wide by a jerk of the head, landed
on the toe of my shoe.

"Kill it," I told Chaim. "It's being eaten alive. What
are you waiting for?"

"I tried," he said. "Listen."

We stood up, and he raised his right foot. The
mouse screeched, faintly, thinly, but audibly, even
above the rustle of the wind in the eucalyptus leaves
above our heads.

"Did you hear that?" said Chaim. "It knows."

"It's because of your shadow."

"My what?"

"The shadow of your foot, which it mistakes for the
shadow of a dangerous animal or a bird. A hawk
perhaps."

"Is that so?"

"Be quick," I told him.

After lunch, we drove the big GMC down to the orchard and unloaded the aluminum bins.

"Why didn't you kill it right away?" I asked him.

"I wanted you to see it."

"Why?"

"*Ai, habibi . . .*" He removed the last bin from the back of the truck and added, "Things like that must happen all the time, don't you think?"

"I imagine so."

"Yes," he said. "But not in the reign of peace."

"The reign of peace?"

"When the Messiah comes." He put the bin down and raised his forefinger. "Not then."

The finger wagged, and I understood. On the flagstone path, under the eucalyptus trees, he had shown me what he expected to be redeemed.

Forcing the End

HAVING REFUSED A CHAIR, RABBI JACOBI STANDS in front of my desk, pulling the tuft of white beard that sprouts beneath his underlip.

"All I want," he says, "is your permission to leave the city, go to Yavneh, open up a school there, and teach."

"Yes, I understand, Rabbi, but unfortunately, under the circumstances, I must refuse you permission."

"What circumstances?"

"For one thing, you'll be safer here."

"Really?" he asks. "Look out the window and tell me what you see."

"Jaffa Road."

"Look again."

I rise to my feet. The street, the entire city has vanished. We are in a wilderness, where a white haze has effaced the boundary between the earth and the azure sky. Mount Scopus is a barren rock, illuminated on its eastern slope by the morning sun. Huge, yellowish limestone boulders, tinged with red, reflect the glaring light. The ruins of buildings? It's impossible to tell. They seem to have been strewn indiscriminately on the parched ground shimmering from the rising heat. Only an ancient, twisted oak, with shriveled leaves, grows there, just below my window, and as I watch, a jackal which has been sleeping in the shade rises unsteadily, its pink tongue lolling from its jaws, and pisses against the tree trunk: a short spurt of urine, in which, suddenly dropping from the cloudless sky, a starling immerses itself for an instant, fluttering its wings and catching a few drops in its gaping beak.

And twisting the tuft of hair below his mouth, Jacobi says, "You're looking at the Holy City through my eyes."

"The past?"

He shrugs. "The future, too. What's the difference? They're one and the same."

"That's impossible."

"Nevertheless, God help us, it's true," he says, covering his face with his hands. As he has been speaking, a Sammael, one of our new, self-propelled rocket launchers, roars up Jaffa Road in the direction of the Russian compound. Its two rockets, capable of carrying nuclear warheads, are covered by canvas.

Jacobi twists that tuft of beard between the thumb and forefinger of his right hand. Is he a hypnotist, or what? I read over his dossier, open on my desk, once again. He was born in Jerusalem in 1917 and was ordained at the age of nineteen. After that, for twelve years, he was the rabbi of the small town of Arav in the southern Galilee, where he also worked as a clerk in the local post office because he refused any remuneration for teaching Torah. His wife died last year, and he lost his only son at the age of sixteen to nephritis. The boy was also a precociously brilliant scholar, of whom his faither said at his death, "I am consoled by the fact that my son, may his memory be blessed, fulfilled the purpose for which man was created—the study of the Holy Law."

For the last eight years, Jacobi has lived in Jerusalem, teaching a select group of students in a small Talmud Torah on Adani Street. He has been in constant conflict with the rabbinate over its acquisition of extensive property, and with the government over its policy of retaliatory raids for terrorist attacks.

My secretary, Dora, whose husband was killed two

years ago by an Arab grenade while serving on re-serve duty in Gaza, comes into my office and whispers excitedly in my ear, "Sunday, at dawn."

"How do you know?"

"Yoram's sister heard it from her husband."

"Who's her husband?"

"The pilot."

"What's the matter with you? You know how tight security is. It's just another rumor."

She adds without conviction, "Yoram's sister swears it's the truth," and sighs. She has aged ex-traordinarily in the last two years; her lips are as wrinkled as an old woman's.

"No, there's still time," Jacobi says. "Not much, but enough. At least enough for me to go to Yavneh, open my school, and plant a few lemon trees. They're very delicate, you know, but I love the odor of the blos-soms, don't you? Sweet but spicy. An unusual com-bination." He goes to the door and says, "Tell me the truth. Do you honestly believe that this time we'll achieve a lasting peace?"

"Absolutely."

"By force of arms?"

"Of course."

"Really? How I admire your faith. Let me tell you something, my friend. A secret. When I'm in Yavneh, and if one day I'm planting a sapling and I hear that the Messiah himself has arrived, do you know what I'll do? Finish planting the sapling, and then go to welcome him." He opens the door. "Did you know that lemons turn yellow only after they've been picked? It's a fact. They remain green and bitter on the tree. You have to store them for months before they turn yellow and ripen."

"Not any more," Dora says. "A specially heated storage plant forces them to ripen in four or five days."

"Is that so? How hot?"

"I'm not sure."

"As hot as this?" he asks, and in the sweaty palm of his right hand he holds up a yellow lemon. "From the new storage plant in Yavneh, by the way, and fully ripe, as you can see; juicy too, with a wonderful smell . . ."

He passes it under Dora's nose.

"Right?" And closing his eyes and inhaling deeply, he recites the traditional benediction, " 'Blessed art Thou—the Eternal, our God, King of the Universe—who hath given fragrance unto fruit.' " Then he smiles, and says, "This one, for your information, was picked from a tree four and a half days ago and then stored at exactly 22° C." He twirls it in the air. "Why, one could almost imagine it's the world: cut off from its source, mercifully ignorant of its state; and just think: some minute malfunction of some machine in that storage plant, for example, or more likely some human error, and the temperature rises only three or four degrees, and look at it now! That marvelous color splotched brown. See? This whole side has changed its color; faintly, but changed, nevertheless, and it's gotten soft—feel it—rotten . . ."

"Where is it?" Dora cries out. "I know. Up your sleeve." But, shaking his head, Jacobi replies, "No, it was only a trick. Well, not exactly that, but . . ."

"What?" she asks, in a peculiar, strident voice that makes Jacobi stare at her. She looks him straight in the eye.

"It's true about you and your brother, isn't it?" he asks, but she says nothing. She and her brother Menachem are reputed to be important members of the Knives, a new, illegal organization allegedly responsible for the murders of a prominent writer who advocated trying to make peace with the Arabs by restoring to them all their territory which we now occupy, and an eighteen-year-old pacifist who, last fall, refused to register for the draft.

Leaving the door open, she goes into the outer office and, with an unlit cigarette dangling from her

wrinkled lips, sits down at her desk and pecks away
with one finger at some official form, in triplicate,
stuffed into her old Remington typewriter. Jacobi follows her. Six of his students from the Talmud Torah
on Adani Street crowd around him, speaking Yiddish
in hushed, agitated voices. One boy, not more than
fifteen, fixes his dark eyes on me and grimaces. He's
deformed in a way I've never seen. His right arm is
normal, but the left, hanging loose, reaches his knee.

Two days later, at about four, while I'm having my
afternoon glass of tea and a butter cookie, I idly
glance out of the window again. Four soldiers, in
battle dress and armed with submachine guns, are
patrolling the street. Each one has inserted a thirty-
round magazine into his weapon, behind the trigger
guard, and has taped another magazine at right an-
gles to the first, to facilitate rapid reloading. Their
footfalls, I notice, are muffled by the sandbags which
last night were heaped up, waist high, against the
walls of the buildings.

Then, at a command from their sergeant, they
break rank, to allow a funeral procession to pass
down the center of the street. Four bearded men,
dressed in black kaftans, are carrying an unpainted
pine coffin on their shoulders. Behind them, three

women, with fringed black shawls over their heads, are howling at the top of their lungs. In spite of the sandbags, the din is terrific. About to shut the window, I notice that the boy with the long arm is also following the coffin. With his good hand, he rhythmically pounds his chest, and his narrow face is twisted by the same grimace he gave me—a grimace that bares his yellow upper teeth to the gums.

"Who is it?" I shout down. "Who's died?" But the howling women, who are now scratching their cheeks with their fingernails, drown me out.

"Answer me," I yell louder, and the boy with the long arm raises his face.

"Our master," he yells back. "The Light of the World."

"Rabbi Jacobi?"

He nods, and Dora, who has been standing behind me, rushes down to the street, where I can see her arguing with one of the pallbearers who has trouble balancing the coffin and rummaging in his pocket for some papers at the same time. When she returns, she says, "They've gotten permission to bury him in Arav."

"Arav?"

"Next to his kid."

"What about transportation?"

"Two horse-drawn carts, if you can believe it."

"Who authorized them to leave the city?"

"What's-his-name. Oh, you know who I mean. That Litvak from the Ministry of Interment who dyes his hair. Kovner."

"Are you sure?"

"Yes," she says. "I'm sure." And she glances at her briefcase, on the filing cabinet, in which she keeps the yellowing document, signed by Kovner, which authorized the burial of her husband, with full military honors, on Mount Herzl.

The next morning, Shmelke Kalb, who works in an office across the street, throws open my door, waving a newspaper in my face. As usual, he's wearing a steel helmet; not because he's the air-raid warden in charge of the block, but because he suffers from skin cancer, a discolored blotch on his forehead, and puts on the helmet whenever he has to go outside, to protect himself from the sun.

"Have you read about Jacobi?" he asks.

"No, but I'm sorry, in a way."

"What're you talking about? Are you crazy? He's deserted the city. And five or six more of his students have already joined him in Yavneh."

"But that's impossible. The man's dead. I saw his funeral procession."

"A sealed coffin?"

"Yes."

"It was a trick to smuggle him out of the city."

"What're you saying?"

"Some of his students nailed him into a coffin and smuggled him out of the city two days ago. It's all here, in this morning's paper, along with some kind of manifesto for some new kind of school he wants to start."

"Let me see that," I tell him, and then read aloud:

We shall be as the disciples of Aaron, loving peace, pursuing peace, and teaching Torah which alone sustains the Jews who, if they faithfully follow its Holy Principles, will be redeemed by them, and then redeem all mankind, in God's good time . . .

Dora has come to the door; Kalb lowers his voice: "They say Kovner has disappeared without a trace."

At one—during critical times like these, we grab a sandwich for lunch at the office—I turn on the radio for the latest news.

". . . which will demand from each of us the greatest sacrifice . . . credence, which, although . . . New York . . ."

I can catch only a word now and then because of the noise: columns of Sammaels, rattling the windowpanes, have been roaring up the street for the last two hours. I twist the knob, and unexpectedly, in a perfectly audible voice, the announcer says that Rabbi Jacobi's body, spattered with dried blood, was discovered in Yavneh early this morning in front of a vegetarian restaurant on the Rishon-Lezion road. A preliminary coroner's report has established that the distinguished religious leader was stabbed once through the heart with a penknife, and died instantly, between 2 and 3 a.m. The district superintendent of police reports that no fingerprints were found on the weapon, but he has been quoted that he is confident that the criminal or criminals will soon be apprehended because of a peculiar aspect of the case. The distinguished rabbi's jaws were pried open after his death, and a yellow lemon inserted in his mouth . . .

Another Sammael, which makes it impossible for me to hear Dora shouting from the outer office, where she's been pecking away at the Remington.

"What?" I ask.

"Green," she says. "The idiot. Not yellow, green."

Going Up

THE TRUCE WITH SYRIA WENT INTO EFFECT AT 6 p.m. At ten, I got a telegram from my uncle Mendel in Jerusalem: "Behold, He who keepeth Israel shall neither slumber nor sleep."

I borrowed a Bible from the kibbutz library and looked it up: it's from Psalm 121. Now that he had retired from the post office with a small pension, Mendel spent most of his time studying the Torah. He would have been completely happy if a widow with whom he had fallen in love had agreed to marry him. I met her only once, the month before, in Jerusalem, where she had inherited a kosher butcher shop on Ben Yehuda Street.

I didn't pay much attention to her. It was a day or so after Nasser had demanded that the U.N. withdraw its observers from Sinai and the Gaza Strip. I had gone to town to scrounge some ammunition from the army for an old German light machine gun we had. The army didn't have any. In case the Syrians attacked, we would have to depend on a Hotchkiss and two Lewis .30-06's. One of the Lewis guns had a defective bolt. You had to be very careful with it. When the bolt slid forward, the damn thing went off by itself.

In any case, the woman remains in my memory standing next to the freshly skinned foreleg of a calf hanging from a hook on the ceiling. The shadow of the hoof falls on her puffy face. Mendel leans toward her across a beef liver in the refrigerated glass counter, and for a few minutes, as we chat, he strokes the back of one of her dry, veined hands.

"How old do you think she is?" he asked me on the way back to his flat.

"It's hard to say."

"Fifty-eight, can you believe it? She looks at least ten years younger, don't you think?"

"She's a handsome woman," I said, and he blushed.

"Did you notice her eyes?" he asked. "The same color as Anna's, may she rest in peace. That's what attracted me to her in the first place."

In his living room, a dog-eared volume of the

Mishna lay open on his desk. Still flushed, he glanced at it for a moment and then, with shining eyes, picked up a slim book, bound in black leather, next to the inkwell.

"Ah . . ."

He sat down and, at his place marked by a slip of paper, began to read. His left hand covered the author's name, but I could see the title impressed in gold: *Tract on Ecstasy.*

"I promised Ruth I'd buy her a pair of sandals," I told him. "I'll be back in about an hour."

Twisting a strand of his beard between his fingers, he continued to read. When I returned, he was stretched out on the horsehair sofa, staring at the ceiling.

"I need her," he said. "I never dreamed I'd marry again, but what can I do? It's a fever in my blood."

"Then marry her."

"I would, if she'd have me. But Yoshe Dressner wants her too."

"Who's Yoshe Dressner?"

"A butcher who used to work for her husband and still helps out in the shop. And he's good. He knows the business. I can't deny it. I don't know anything about running a butcher shop." He sat up. "Still, she's a vigorous woman and needs a vigorous man, like me.

Not an *alter kocker* like Dressner," he lapsed furiously into Yiddish. "An old fart of sixty-nine with arthritis."

He sighed, leaned back, and closed his eyes. His face was suddenly ugly from exhaustion: yellowish and drained.

"Do you think there's going to be another war?" he asked me.

"I don't know. I hope not."

"What about the U.N.?"

"What good is the U.N.?"

"Yes," he said. "What can we expect from the goyim?"

"How about a bite to eat?" I asked him. "There must be a good kosher restaurant around here. What do you say? It's on me."

"No, I'm not hungry," he said. "But you go ahead."

It was getting dark. He switched on his goose-necked lamp, sat down, and, with his elbows on the desk, resumed reading. By the time I left to catch the 7 p.m. bus to the Galilee, the color had seeped back into his cheeks; his ears and the tip of his nose were bright red. It was as though the fever in his blood had abated for a while, and then risen again.

He had been an *iluy*, a prodigy who was an accomplished Talmudic scholar at eight, and in his teens, the most brilliant student at his yeshiva in Warsaw. But at eighteen, when he married my mother's sister, Anna, he went to work for his father-in-law.

"He had a hardware store," he once told me. "A hole in the wall on Okopowa Street, right opposite the cemetery. We sold a little of everything. Nails, pots and pans, knives, coal, oil. You name it. We had to work ten, twelve hours a day just to make ends meet. My father-in-law, may he rest in peace, was getting old and needed my help, but he begged me to quit and go back to studying. 'You could become a famous rabbi,' he said. 'Rich and respected.' But that was the point. How could I do a thing like that? Make a profit from teaching what God has given freely to the Jews? God forbid! Anna understood; not a word of complaint from her, ever, may God rest her soul."

They couldn't have children, and when I was born, they loved me like their own. I was the reason they followed my parents to Palestine in 1932. My father was originally a trade-union organizer for the Jewish Bund, but he realized there wasn't any future for Jews in Poland, became a Zionist, and emigrated. He worked for the Jewish Agency in Jerusalem and got Mendel a job selling stamps at the main post office on Jaffa Road. When my parents died within eight months of each other in 1946, I went to live with him and Anna in their two-room flat over a Hungarian restaurant on King George Street.

Neither of them ever tried to impose their belief on me. I was a socialist, like my father, and in the summer of 1949, when I joined the kibbutz, they raised no objections. Mendel said, "We'll come and visit you." Apart from attending my wedding in 1952, they never did.

Then, on the morning after the truce, at nine, he arrived, unannounced. He had bummed a lift on a truck carrying drums of machine oil as far as Afula, and another in an army jeep to Kiriat Shemona. It was a Saturday—the first time I had known him to travel on the Sabbath.

"God forgive me," he said. "I couldn't help it. I had to see if you and Ruth were okay."

"We're fine."

"God be praised." He put down his cardboard suitcase, solemnly shook my hand, and said, "All honor to you." It's a biblical salutation which is used in modern Hebrew to congratulate a soldier on a successful mission.

"Thank you."

Ruth chewed her lower lip. She had just spent six days and nights in a shelter, under fire, and now had to help clean up the mess: hose down the concrete floor and walls, empty the chemical latrines, air the straw mattresses. Her eyes were red and swollen— she had been averaging three hours' sleep a night— but we would have to give up our bed to our guest and sleep on those itchy mattresses on the floor of our room.

There was nothing else we could do. Mendel was sixty-six—his white beard made him look even older —and the trip had almost finished him off: he had walked the two kilometers from Kiriat Shemona to the kibbutz lugging that cardboard suitcase in the broiling sun. He sat down wearily on the bed and carefully laid out the contents beside him: two pairs of underwear and socks, two shirts, a toothbrush, a plastic comb, and two knives, two forks, two spoons, and two plates wrapped in newspaper—one of each for meat and the other for dairy dishes—along with four cans of kosher beef stew, six jars of sour cream, phylacteries in a red velvet bag, a silk prayer shawl, a prayer book, and a volume of the Mishna.

"What about your *Tract on Ecstasy*?" I asked him.

"What? Oh. I left that at home. It's very difficult, you see, and required enormous effort." He patted the volume of the Mishna with affection as if, like an old, beloved dog, it was incapable of surprising him and would never turn. "There are ecstasies and ecstasies," he said. "One must be very careful to distinguish between them."

He gazed with bleary eyes around the room and suddenly went on, "You might as well know it now. Hemda is going to marry Dressner on the twentieth of next month."

"I'm sorry to hear it," I told him.

"Yes," he said. "I'm sorry too." Then, rubbing his hands together, he smiled. "*Nu*, what are you waiting for? Aren't you going to show me around?"

"There's not much to see."

"Where were you during the fighting?"

"Manning the Hotchkiss in a trench next to the command bunker."

"You must have seen the whole battle for the Golan Heights."

"We were being shelled. I kept my head down most of the time. Once in a while, I took a peep through my binoculars."

"What was it like?"

"I can probably borrow our jeep and take you up tomorrow if you like. That'll give you some idea."

"Wonderful."

"Now take a shower and get some rest," I told him.

"No," he insisted. "First show me around." So I took him on a fast tour of the kibbutz.

"Not one direct hit?" he kept repeating in astonishment.

"Not one."

He stared at the crater made by a 120 mm. shell which had exploded on the road about ten meters from the garage where I worked.

"It's a miracle," he said.

The view, that night, of the Golan Heights left him speechless. It was something to which none of us, as yet, had become accustomed. The moon, in its first quarter, had just risen and in its feeble light the mountains looked flat and dark. The lights of the Syrian fortifications on the slopes had been extinguished—for the first time in twenty years. We went back to our room, where Ruth was putting away some of my freshly laundered shirts.

"Did you get my telegram?" Mendel asked me.

"Yes."

"You don't pray, of course, but those particular words from the Psalm are part of the prayer that's recited before going to sleep," he said. "It's a good time to pray. The body is tired but the mind is ex-traordinarily clear. Do you know the feeling? Your thoughts echo, and sometimes it seems they carry very far. I don't think I ever prayed as hard as in the last month, even when Anna got sick . . ."

"Coffee?" Ruth asked him.

"I forgot to bring a cup," he said, and he blushed —this time from embarrassment. He was afraid that the few dishes we kept in our room for snacks might be contaminated by having been used for both meat and dairy.

"We only use the cups for coffee," I told him.

"Never soup?"

"Never."

"Then a cup of coffee, by all means," he said. "Thank you." But he stirred the sugar with his own spoon.

"It was wonderful being in Jerusalem last week," he went on. "Did you know that our troops were ordered to attack the Old City through the Dung Gate but refused? Instead, they attacked through Saint Stephen's, in the eastern wall. They felt it was more dignified. And they were right; they were right. Did you ever imagine that you would live to see all Jerusalem in our hands again? I never did. It seems so strange and mysterious. Have you heard about the paratrooper crying at the Western Wall? Someone asked him why, and he said it was because he was from a kibbutz, and no one had ever taught him how to pray. It's a true story. I heard it from Hershel Glick, who was there. Do you remember Hershel Glick? No matter. He was there and swears it's true. Sentimental, I know, but true. It seems like a dream, doesn't it? In the sense that it all has a hidden meaning you can't quite grasp. And, of course, it does . . ."

He sipped his coffee. Ruth lit a cigarette. I was astonished she didn't argue with him. Then she said to me, "At least they're alive."

"Yes, that's something."

She was talking about three members of the kibbutz who had been wounded in action and were in the Hadassah Hospital in Jerusalem.

"Yora, you know, hasn't heard anything about Asher since Thursday morning," she said.

"I know."

She puffed on the cigarette and watched the smoke drift through the screen door. Her eyes swam with tears; it was as if she were witnessing the dissipation of hope.

"Who's Asher?" Mendel asked me.

"Asher Goldmann, one of our members. He's been

reported missing in action at Sheikh Zuweid. Ruth and his wife are good friends. They work together in the laundry. She's a painter."

I pointed to the picture of a pink peony hung over our bed. It was one of a dozen she had done in oils of the flowers, shrubs, and trees we'd planted around the kibbutz over the years.

"It's like a photograph," said Mendel with admiration. "Amazing. That dew drop on the petal looks real. She's a talented girl. How old is she?"

"Twenty."

"Very talented," he repeated. "You'd swear it was an enlarged photograph."

Ruth said, "Asher's going to be twenty-one in November."

"He's a good kid," I said, and I meant it. He was built like an ox and worked very hard in our apple orchard.

The next day was an ordinary working day. I lubricated our two GMC's in the garage, Ruth and Yora ironed shirts in the laundry, and twenty extra men were assigned to our cotton fields, which hadn't been weeded or irrigated in six days. It was touch and go whether we'd be able to save the crop. There was good news from Hadassah Hospital; none of the three had been seriously wounded. But there was still no news about Goldmann.

After lunch I caught a glimpse of Yora leaving the dining hall. She had a fixed smile on her lips—or a grimace, baring her teeth, which resembled a smile and made you instinctively respond with a grin.

Mendel spent the day in our room studying the Mishna. When I came back from work at four, I said, "Come on outside and get a breath of fresh air."

But there was no breeze; it was stifling. We sat out on the lawn in the lengthening shadow of a poplar tree.

After supper, we learned that Goldmann was dead. His commander had telephoned Yora from Jerusalem, offered his condolences, and informed her that her husband had been temporarily interred in a military cemetery outside Tel Aviv. If she wished, he would be exhumed and reburied on the kibbutz.

At ten, Yora came to our room, wavered, and sat down, unsteadily, in the wicker chair. I thought she was drunk: she had trouble keeping her eyes open, and her speech was slurred.

"They gave me two phenobarbs in the infirmary," she explained. "With a glass of warm water. Acts very fast. I never took phenobarb before."

Ruth said, "Come. I'll put you to bed."

"No, no. First, I want to speak with Shlomo. Only for a moment. Do you mind?" she asked me.

"Of course not."

Her head lolled back against the whitewashed wall, she licked her lips, and with her eyes shut, she said, "That's very kind. You fought up here, in the Galilee, during the War of Independence, didn't you?"

"Yes, with the New Brigade, at Safsaf and Jish."

"Were there many losses?"

"Things were very rough at Jish."

"And the dead," she said, trying to focus her blurred eyes on me. "Is that where they buried them?"

"I can't remember. I suppose so, but I imagine they exhumed later and sent home."

"And did you see any of the bodies which had been exhumed?"

"No."

"Would you do me a favor?"

"If I can."

"I want to have Asher cremated immediately. Can you arrange that?"

"I can try."

"I'd appreciate it." She yawned until her jaws cracked. "Excuse me."

"That's okay."

"He wasn't good-looking," she said. "He had a bad

complexion. But he had a beautiful body, don't you think? I thought so. Those broad shoulders and narrow hips. No hair on his chest. I've never cared for hairy men." She yawned again. "I don't want him exhumed. The coffin will be sealed, I know, but I prefer cremation. Immediate cremation, if it can be arranged.

"He was a beautiful boy," she said. "At least he was to me. He slept on his stomach. Or rather, he fell asleep on his stomach, but in the morning would always be lying on his back with both hands on his balls—if you'll pardon the expression—and the happiest grin on his face."

"Come to bed," Ruth repeated.

"A good idea." The girl rose and staggered forward, bumping her knee against a corner of my Grundig short-wave radio on the low table in the center of the room. "Excuse me," she said, and staggered again. Mendel reached out his hands to steady her, but she waved him off. At the door, with her left cheek pressed against the screen, she said, "I much prefer the fire. I have that kind of mind. It can't be helped. A mind for details. All kinds of details. I can't help imagining what's happening to him." She turned the doorknob, which squeaked. "Just in the natural course of things, as we say."

"Here, put your arm around my neck," said Ruth. "That's a good girl."

"I hope to God I can sleep. I haven't had a wink of sleep in seventy-two hours."

"Of course you will," Ruth said. "You'll sleep like a baby," and when they were outside on the flagstone porch in the dark, she called out, "Be careful of the steps."

She came back at eleven. Mendel said, "It makes me very sad."

"Why should it?" Ruth asked him. "Don't you believe in life after death?"

"I don't think much about it, to be honest. Didn't the Besht, may his name be blessed, once say: 'If I love God, I have no need of life after death'?"

"*Hara*," said Ruth in Arabic. "Shit."

The following morning, I tried twice to put a telephone call through to a buddy of mine at G.H.Q. in Jerusalem and arrange the cremation. It was impossible. All the lines were jammed. The operator suggested that I try again tomorrow afternoon.

It was a very hot day, and dry. The air was so dry your sweat evaporated almost instantaneously. I overhauled the engine of one of our John Deere tractors in the garage, where the sun beat down on the corrugated metal roof.

At four, I got the use of our jeep for two hours. Ruth said it was too hot to take Mendel up, but he was adamant. She found him a straw hat with a wide brim and we took off.

I followed the path of the assault three days before: the rutted dirt track, marked by tank treads, behind Kfar Szold, which leads up the slope. It was so steep I had to stay in first and use four-wheel drive all the way. The wheels churned up a thick cloud of red dust that hung in the air around us.

Then I slowed down a little. Right below us was a white shack: OP Alpha, the abandoned U.N. Observation Post. The door had been left open. We were in Syria, or what had formerly been Syria.

"Go on," Mendel said. "Keep going. I'm choking to death." But after a few hundred meters, he grabbed my arm and shouted above the roar of the engine, "Ours?"

Just off the road, on the right, there was a Ford half-track—a troop carrier—which had taken a direct hit through the armored door next to the driver's seat, exploded, and burned. The barrel of the forward machine gun had buckled from the heat.

"Is it ours?" Mendel repeated.

"Yes."

"I can't breathe."

At the top of the plateau, I pulled up. The dust settled, the sun gleamed on some spent 50-caliber cartridges scattered ahead of us along the blistered asphalt road.

"Where does the road go?" Mendel asked.

"Straight to Damascus."

"We're in Syria?" He raised himself up, grasping the windshield, and gazed around him at the wheat fields strewn with black basalt boulders pitted like meteorites.

"At least they could have planted trees by the road," he said. "Something green. A little shade." And as he sat down again, the dry stalks of wheat rustled in a hot breeze. He held his nose and said, "Heavenly father! Where are the bodies?"

"In those fields."

"Why don't we bury them?"

"Do you want to go back?"

He shook his head, so I drove about three kilometers more on that vast plain while he held his nose and his beard fluttered in the wind. He looked younger. The dust had colored his beard a reddish-brown and, like makeup, had covered the wrinkles on his forehead and at the corners of his eyes.

"Did you see that?" he called out. "The dog lying there? Its eyes were wide open."

I slowed down to avoid the swollen carcass of a gray donkey on its back. Its belly was enormous. Then there was another one, in a leather harness, and beside it, a bloated cow and her calf with a black and white face. Its belly had burst open; the entrails coiled on the road.

"The Torah forbids it," Mendel said. "It's forbidden to slaughter a cow and her calf on the same day."

There were two more dead cows, another donkey, and a reddish cow with a white face and markings on its flank. It looked like a pure-bred Hereford to me.

"Wait," said Mendel. "Stop."

Just ahead of us was a barefoot Syrian boy wearing a white shirt and faded blue pants. He was lying on his right side, his head resting on his outstretched right arm.

"Is he asleep?" Mendel asked.

"No."

"How can you be so sure? His eyes are closed. He looks asleep to me," he said, and before I could stop him, he bolted out of the jeep. I went after him and, with my foot, turned the corpse on its back. It was getting ripe. The bloated face was very pale, but there was a reddish-blue blotch on the right cheek and another one on his throat.

"He wasn't a soldier," said Mendel. "He was too young for that. He can't be more than seventeen. What's he doing here? Why didn't he run away?"

"I have no idea."

"Was he married, do you think?"

"I doubt it. He was a peasant. They have to pay a bride-price, and it usually takes them years to save it up. Why do you ask?"

"I was just thinking. I was about the same age when I met Anna," he said, with his eyes fixed on the bloated face.

He crouched down. "Did you hear that? He's alive. He just belched."

"It's gas."

"Gas?"

"He's beginning to swell up."

"Are you sure?" he asked. "But what killed him? I don't see any blood."

"It's hard to say. Concussion, probably, from a shell. Yes, there's the crater over there. You see it? Near the road, where the wheat's been burned away?"

"A shell?" he repeated. "Theirs or ours?"

"What difference does it make?"

He looked up at me—his eyes were bloodshot from the dust—but said nothing.

And for half an hour after we got back to the kibbutz, he remained silent. We showered and changed our clothes. I fiddled with my short-wave and picked up the BBC World Service; a rebroadcast of a concert from the Albert Hall, in which it was hard to distinguish the applause and the Brahms from the crackling static. Mendel took down the borrowed Bible from the shelf above my bed and, seated in the wicker chair, read and reread a single page, mouthing the words under his breath.

Once, he said aloud, "It's a beautiful Psalm."

"Which?"

"The hundred and twenty-first. And you know something? I believe it. I'm sixty-six years old, I've been around, but I believe it. He sees everything." He stroked his damp beard. "He never sleeps. One forgets. It wouldn't be so bad if I believed He was asleep."

Lamentations

I'M THREE MONTHS PREGNANT," SAID ELANA. "URI is going to be a father."

Yigael, who had been waiting for this all through dinner, drank off the rest of his brandy, and said, "He told me. *Mazel tov.*"

"Thank you. I found out the day after you were called up, but I couldn't decide whether to write him about it or not. He had enough to worry about out there."

"You did the right thing. It made him very happy."

"Did it?" she asked eagerly.

"Very."

"I'm so glad. I couldn't tell from his last letter. He asked me to marry him, of course, but almost as an afterthought. Most of it was about one of his men who had been blinded by a piece of shrapnel the day before."

"Avner Levi."

"That's the one."

"He and Uri were friends at law school," said Yigael. "Believe me, under the circumstances, Uri was very happy. He asked me to be his best man."

"Then do," Elana said.

"I don't understand."

"It's very simple. I want the child to have his name, so I spoke with the chaplain of your outfit, who fixed it with the rabbinate. We're getting married next Thursday afternoon at Bet Hakerem."

"In the cemetery?"

"Over his grave," Elana said. "I insisted on it."

Yigael tried to imagine the scene. Would there be a *chuppah*? A canopy erected over the mound of fresh earth? And who would speak for the dead? Slip the ring on the girl's finger and then smash the glass underfoot?

"Can you make it?" she asked.

"Yes, I think so. I'll get Ginzberg to take my afternoon class."

"Good. It'll be a very small affair. Just the immediate family and you," she said, licking her spoon.

"How about a cup of coffee?"

"It's too warm. But another ice cream would be nice."

"More chocolate?"

"Make it vanilla this time."

"Waiter, a dish of vanilla ice cream," Yigael called out. "And bring me another brandy. A double."

"Some water, too."

"And two glasses of cold water."

"I'm simply ravenous all the time," Elana said.

"No morning sickness?"

"Not a bit of it. The only symptom I have is sore breasts. My nipples are very tender."

The waiter carried the dish of ice cream, the snifter of brandy, and two glasses of cloudy water to the table on a big aluminum tray. He was about fifty, tall, stooped, and surprisingly fast on his feet for a cripple who dragged his right leg. The glasses were filled to the brim, but he set them down on the table without spilling a drop. Although he had obviously been a waiter for some time, he seemed absurdly out of place among the soiled tablecloths, waxed-paper napkins, and potted palms with wilting fronds that stood about the room. With his straw-colored, untrimmed beard, his earlocks, the yarmulke on the bald crown of his head, he looked to Yigael as if he had wandered in here by mistake on his way to one of the dark, smelly synagogues in Mea Shearim.

"What's this?" Yigael asked him.

"What's it look like? It's your check."

"What's the rush?"

"You call yourself a Jew? Tonight's the beginning of Tisha b'Av."

"What is it?" asked Elana, who had been concentrating on her ice cream.

"Tisha b'Av," Yigael repeated, sipping his brandy.

"Is that so? Do you fast?" she asked the waiter, and explained to Yigael, "My grandfather always fasted on Tisha b'Av and slept with his head on a stone."

"In this country?"

"On the floor of his apartment on Herzl Street, in Tel Aviv."

"There's something peculiar about the whole thing," said Yigael.

"What do you mean?"

"Think about it for a moment. What's the literal meaning of Tisha b'Av?"

"The ninth day of the Hebrew month of Av," said Elana.

"Well, according to the Second Book of Kings, the Babylonians burned down Jerusalem and the temple on the seventh of Av, but Jeremiah says it happened on the tenth."

"So what?"

"Don't you see? Why fast on the ninth? It's the wrong day." He swirled the brandy in the snifter grasped in his hand. "The Talmud has some elaborate explanation, but I forget what it is." He swallowed the brandy. "There's some evidence that the ninth of Av was a Babylonian festival the Jews picked up during the exile there."

"What kind of festival?"

"Something to do with the death of Tammuz, I think—the god of fertility. In any case, the Jews apparently adapted it for their own purposes."

"Listen, Mister, how about the check? It's almost sundown. I've got to go to shul," the waiter insisted. He spoke Hebrew with a strong Polish-Yiddish accent.

"Where're you from?" Yigael asked as he paid up.

"Here and there."

"Warsaw?"

"Yes, Warsaw, too," the waiter said. "Why?"

"My father came from Warsaw."

"Oh?" The waiter stopped fumbling in his pocket for the change and looked at Yigael with interest for the first time. "Was he there during the war?"

"No, he came here in 1932."

149

"Lucky."

"Not at all," said Yigael. "Smart. He was a Zionist."

"And his family?"

"They stayed in Warsaw and were killed during the war."

"In the ghetto?"

"In Auschwitz."

"What was their name?"

"Janower."

"I knew a Rabbi Lazer Janower in Auschwitz," the waiter said. "A great Talmudic scholar. But he was from Vilna. Any relation?"

"Not that I know," said Yigael, unable to keep the contempt out of his voice. He had met this type before—the kind who had undoubtedly been deported without protest, who, at night in the barracks, had never failed to gratefully mumble the blessing over a crust of moldy bread. His yellowish, bloodshot eyes had seen in the heaps of naked corpses the will of God.

"That's O.K. Forget it. Keep the change," Yigael said, waving him away in disgust.

The man shambled off, the tray under one arm, dragging his right foot. His rubber heel left a black streak on the tiles between the wilting potted palms. Elana was again licking her spoon with the greediness of a child. Yigael closed his eyes. The double brandy had gone right to his head and made him sweat. It was too damn hot to drink. Jerusalem was having a particularly hot summer, and now, to top it off, the newspapers were predicting a khamsin. Maybe it had already begun. The restaurant was stifling. There was the smell of burned fat in the air. Had there been a fire in the kitchen?

"Do you smell something burning?" he asked Elana. She shook her head, and, sure enough, when Yigael sniffed the air again he detected nothing. It was a trick of the mind, he realized. The brandy stinging his tongue, the heat, the sweat trickling down between his shoulder blades had evoked the smell of fatty sausages frying in a pan over a portable gas stove. He was with his reserve unit again, on the canal, opposite Ismailia, in an underground bunker where the sausages sizzled and a bottle of Remy Martin was being passed from hand to hand. It was a celebration. For almost twenty minutes now, there had been a lull in the Egyptian barrage, which had begun at dawn, four hours before. The bottle was passed to him again. There was one good swallow left. He decided to save it for Uri, who was in command of a communications bunker a kilometer up the line.

And then standing on the steps was the red-headed medic from Haifa, who in the last week had developed a twitch in his left eyelid.

"Yigael, it's Uri. You'd better come . . ."

"What happened?"

"A fluke," the medic said. "One of those things. He was in the slit trench, on his way back from the latrine, when the attack started."

"Is he dead?"

The eyelid twitched. "The first shell. A one-twenty-two from a howitzer."

The lid twitched again, and he added plaintively, "We did all we could. We found all of him except the right arm below the elbow."

The waiter reemerged from the kitchen and began to scrape and clack his way on the tiles across the room; he had replaced his shoes with wooden-soled slippers. Elana eyed him curiously over the glass of water raised to her lips and said, "My grandfather used to wear those things to go to synagogue on Tisha b'Av, too. Why do religious Jews take off their shoes when they mourn?"

"What's the difference?"

"It makes no sense to me."

"Tisha b'Av makes no sense," said Yigael. "Not any more. There's no need for it any more." And he watched the man leave the restaurant through the glass door and turn down Jaffa Road. The door remained ajar; for a moment after the man was out of sight, the scrape and clack of his wooden soles still grated on Yigael's ears: an echo from the past—like the man himself, who was limping off to mourn the destruction of a city that had been rebuilt and an exile that had finally been brought to an end.

"It's easy to see why you and Uri were so close," Elana said.

"We grew up together."

"It's much more than that. He didn't read poetry as a rule, but he was always quoting . . . Is it Shlonsky?"

Yigael's attention had momentarily strayed back to the glass door. The setting sun flashed on a window above the pharmacy across the street; a scrap of paper fluttered against the curb. Then the verse she was reciting caught at him:

> There is no angel there.
> The boy must free himself
> And seize the knife,

Bind up his father,
Throw the altar down.

There is no Covenant.
The sacrifice we make
Is for a portion promised us
By no one but ourselves.

"No, it's not by Shlonsky," said Yigael. "I can't re-member who wrote it. Maybe Lamdan."

"It makes no difference. It meant a great deal to him. It was the only poem he knew by heart." She smiled dimly. "He taught it to me one night last win-ter when he was drunk. But you know something?" she added. "For the life of me, I can't remember the sound of his voice. Can you imagine that? He's only been dead six weeks."

"That's perfectly natural."

"Is it really? I didn't know."

He stared at her in amazement, and with envy. After all, she was twenty-three. She had been born here, had lived through three wars, but up till now had somehow managed to escape unscathed. He re-sented her luck. At her age, he had already buried his father and at least three good friends. His father had been killed in the fight for Jish, up north, in 1948. All

that remained of him in Yigael's memory were his
bushy mustache, prematurely streaked with gray, and
a pair of round, steel-rimmed glasses.

He rose unsteadily to his feet. "Come on," he said.
"You must be tired. I'll take you home."

As they crossed the Street of the Prophets, a dry,
hot wind, laden with dust, blew in their faces—the
khamsin, at last, from the Wilderness of Judea, carrying with it a faint odor of scorched wild flowers and
withered grass. The particles of dust streamed in the
headlights of a passing car. Yigael coughed; the girl
stumbled and clutched at his arm. A strand of her
hair, which brushed his cheek, was already damp and
tangled with sweat.

They continued up Strauss Street. At the entrance
to the hospital, a Home Guard, with a Lee-Enfield
slung awkwardly over one shoulder, sucked furiously
on his unlit pipe. He had wrinkled lips, white eyebrows. Ten years too old for the active reserve, he had
been called up, thought Yigael, to protect those only
a little more defenseless than himself.

There was a small synagogue on the next corner.
Yigael glanced through an open window on the
ground floor. Elana, who lived up the block, tugged
at his sleeve, but the sight held him: the Ark and the

bimah draped in black cloth, the overturned benches, the fifteen or twenty men seated in a dim circle of light on the stone floor. Their shadows wavered on the wall. All the lights in the place had been extinguished, Yigael realized, except for the brass oil lamp suspended from the ceiling on a chain before the Ark. The wick smoked.

Elana pulled again at his sleeve. "In a minute," said Yigael. An old man on the *bimah* was chanting from the Book of Lamentations in a nasal voice: " 'Jerusalem remembereth in the days of her affliction and her anguish all her treasures that she had in the days of old . . .' "

"I've got to get home," said Elana. "I've got to take a shower. I'm all in." The urgency of her tone made Yigael look at her. Her face was streaming with sweat. "It's the damn khamsin," she explained. "It always gets on my nerves. Uri once told me that when the Turks were here their judges were very lenient with people who committed crimes during a khamsin." She ran her fingers through her stringy hair and rambled on, "He was thinking of doing a book on the administration of Ottoman law in Palestine—did you know that? It interested him very much. He had already done some of the research. I have his notes."

The wind had dropped a little; the nasal chant in the synagogue rose.

"We lived together almost six months," said Elana. "I gave away all his clothes. One loose-leaf notebook and a few of his letters are all I have left."

"You'll have the child," said Yigael.

"Yes. I'm counting on that." Her face still shone with sweat, but she seemed calmer, as if her anxiety had diminished with the wind. "By the way, the wedding is at three. My parents have hired a car. We can pick you up at the university, if you like."

"That'd be fine," Yigael said. "What about the ring?"

"All taken care of. I bought one last week in a little shop on Ben Yehuda. Fourteen-carat gold, and wide —I like wide wedding bands—but very reasonable."

A wide gold band. It was something Yigael could easily visualize, and with it he pictured a wineglass wrapped in a white handkerchief, and, for some reason, a fringed *chuppah*, embroidered with roses, casting its shadow on the grave.

"Did you invite Levi?" he asked.

"Will he be out of the hospital?"

"No, but he'd appreciate an invitation."

"I'll write him tomorrow."

On the *bimah*, the old man blew his nose into his fingers, and, as Yigael turned away, resumed his nasal chant: " 'Zion spreadeth forth her hands, and there is none to comfort her . . .' "

"We'll pick you up at two in front of the library," said Elana. "Is that O.K.?"

"Yes," Yigael said, but his voice broke, and he averted his face, astonished by the tears that welled up in his eyes.